Miniature Shops

Also by MARGARET B. DUDA

Dollhouse Accessories: How To Design and Make Them

Photography by

Joe Vigliano *and* Jon Sheckler

Miniature Shops

How To Design and Make Them

Margaret B. Duda

South Brunswick and New York: A. S. Barnes and Company
London: Thomas Yoseloff Ltd

A. S. Barnes and Co., Inc.
Cranbury, New Jersey 08512

Thomas Yoseloff Ltd
Magdalen House
136-148 Tooley Street
London SE1 2TT, England

Library of Congress Cataloging in Publication Data

Duda, Margaret B.
Miniature shops.

Bibliography: p.
Includes index.
1. Miniature craft. 2. Shops, Retail—Models.
I. Title.
TT178.D82 1977 745.59'28 76-10884
ISBN 0-498-01783-4

PRINTED IN THE UNITED STATES OF AMERICA

to
John Duda, Jr.,
my father-in-law,
with gratitude

Contents

Acknowledgments
Introduction

1	Basic Box and Accessories	17
2	General Store	30
3	1899 Toy Shop	61
4	1915 Confectionery	93
5	Victorian Millinery	119
6	1861 One-Room Schoolhouse	140
7	Shop Fronts	160

Bibliography 168
Index 169

Acknowledgments

I would like to extend my gratitude to Joe Vigliano and Jon Sheckler for their creativity and patience in photographing my miniatures; to Don Spooner for his meticulous drawings; to John Duda, Jr., my father-in-law, whose craftsmanship added a great deal to my book; and to my husband, Larry, and my four children, David, John, Paul, and Laura, who agreed to share my time with yet another book.

Introduction

Miniature shops have been popular for over two hundred years. Some of the earliest ones on record are the "nine shops of the marketplace filled with little figures of enamel," which belonged to the little Dauphin, grandson of Louis XIV, in 1696, and were recorded in the Inventory of the Crown. Soon after that, we find records of almost a hundred box rooms showing a village and details of daily court life built from 1716 to 1750 for Princess Augusta Dorothea in Schwarzburg-Arnstadt. Like the dollhouses, the earliest samples of miniature shops were owned by royalty, but by the nineteenth century, they were being made for the common lover of miniatures.

By the mid-eighteen hundreds, we see fine examples of the specialty shops that were common in that period. The English were especially fond of butcher shops, and the Cooper Union Museum of New York City has such a miniature shop that is complete with sides of beef hanging in the open air and a proprietor in a top hat. The Museum of the City of New York has a late nineteenth-century draper's shop where bolts of cloth with price tags are piled on shelves and samples are displayed in the front windows. There were other kinds of stores as well, such as milliner shops with stands lined with feathered and flowered hats, toy shops filled with childhood dreams of the period, bakery shops and delicatessens, greengrocers and sweet shops, and of course, the most varied of all stores, the general store, although these early ones were not as elaborate as their contemporary counterparts.

These miniature shops have survived to tell us how people shopped hundreds of years ago. While most of them probably started out as a child's toy, they are now all collector's items. Miniaturists are taking the hint. Antique collectors are grabbing miniature stores found in antique shops. Others are using their travels to find souvenirs for elaborate Oriental and china shops.

As a young mother, I found that I could neither afford the prices in antique shops, nor did I travel to exotic places that sell unusual miniatures. This did not stop me from wanting a shop, however, since I have always felt that a miniature scene in perfect scale is a real work of art. Unfortunately, it was at this time that we discovered our twin sons needed braces and buying a shop, even a contemporary one, was discouraged. Since I had recently furnished my daughter's dollhouse for a book, I looked into the possibility of creating miniature shops and writing a book about them.

I went to the library and looked for books on period shops. I found other fine examples in our postcard collection. The shops from the 1800s seemed to be the most fascinating, and I decided on a general store after a visit to the Smithsonian. It was there that I also found the confectionery and the one-room schoolhouse. The toy shop and millinery were decided on later as I became intrigued with the possibilities for miniature toys and hats.

I now knew what I wanted but not how to build it. I liked the idea that a miniature shop did not take as much room as a dollhouse. This was a major consideration with four children in the house. I finally decided to make three-sided boxes like the ones that were popular with German and French collectors, as well as the Victorian Americans. These could be either hung on a wall or set on a bookshelf. As I thought about it, I discovered that the same basic box could be used for all the shops and even the schoolroom, which would make it easier to construct them on an assembly line basis.

Looking at pictures of period shops, I slowly devised ways to make the furnishings and accessories. My father-in-law came to the rescue with the harder pieces, as well as with the fronts for the shops discussed in the last chapter. The shops slowly took shape. I did find that I would finish a shop and then have to return to it as I found a way to make yet another accessory. I realized that it must be for this reason that deadlines are placed on writers. I could have gone on forever, I think, if I had not had the deadline to contain my enthusiasm.

As you will notice in the pictures of the completed shops, I am not a purist in the sense that I will allow store-bought items in my scenes if they seem to add to the overall impression. Some items were gifts from friends, others were pieces I felt were necessary but could not make, such as the metal and glass objects.

I am sure that I will add to the shops for years to come as I think of items I forgot or find new ways to make additions. That is one of the great advantages of a shop over a dollhouse. There is only so much you can put into a room setting without having it look crowded, while you can keep adding to a shop to make it look more interesting. You may want to rearrange our furnishings and accessories to fit your own scheme. You can use different materials and different colors. You may even find simpler ways to construct some of the items. However you make the shops, you will certainly find that you are creating pleasure for yourself and an heirloom for your descendants, for as A.C. Benson says in *The Book of the Queen's Dolls' House*: "There is great beauty in smallness."

Miniature Shops

1

Basic Box and Accessories

Before you think of a particular store, you will have to think of every store. What turns a miniature room into a store? Better yet, what type of room makes a store?

The nineteenth-century shops were usually a single room, and you will find all you need in a simple, three-sided shadow box, which was so popular during the last century. From this basic box, you may want to go on and build a more elaborate structure. Some miniaturists prefer to put lengths of wood across the top, simulating rafters. This is especially good for the general store since you can then hang things from these rafters as they often did in the real stores. Others might want to put a ceiling on the store and a framed glass front that hinges from the top for easy accessibility. These are charming since they keep the miniatures dust free, but they also make the rooms much darker. To alleviate this, you could also have a clear glass top or you could install lighting in the ceiling. Some miniaturists use small Christmas tree lights attached behind the rafters or along the edge of the ceiling. Others use HO lighting systems. One miniaturist cut a hole in the ceiling for a small, florescent fixture and hid this with yet another cover, making a false ceiling in the box. Still another possibility is the one we finally chose. We set some of the boxes in our built-in bookshelves and put lighting fixtures beneath the shelves above them. We then hinged the fronts of the shops described in the last chapter onto the fronts of the boxes. This way we could turn on the lights and the viewer could look in through the windows, which are at eye level, or the fronts could be removed for a better view. The possibilities are as endless as your imagination.

Once you have your shadow box, you still don't have a store. Even with paint and a planked floor, you still have only a room that could be a bedroom as well as a general store. To turn a room into a shop, you will need shelves and counters and a cash register and a clock and all of those necessities that were common to every store of the late nineteenth century.

You will need either plywood or hardwood planed down to size for the shadow box. Basswood or balsa wood may be used for the furnishings. Balsa wood may be cut with an X-acto knife you can purchase in a hobby shop, while more elaborate tools are necessary for the basswood. The basswood will last longer, however, and may be ordered in quantity from such places as Craftsman Wood Service Co., 2727 S. Mary St., Chicago, Illinois 60608. You may stain the furnishings as we did or paint them for more color or leave them natural with a coat of varnish for durability.

There will be many other necessities for the individual stores, but these will be mentioned in the chapter that deals with that shop. For instance, a crate would certainly go into a general store, but not a millinery. A tool bench is needed in the toymaker's workshop, but not in the confectionery.

You may also find that you will want more of one kind of furnishing than another for a particular store. For instance, you could use two showcases instead of counters in the sweet shop for the baked goods. The choice will be up to you and the needs of your store. Plan ahead and then go ahead and follow our simple instructions for the basic structures.

Basic Construction Layout

The first thing you will need is a basic structure to house your shop, no matter which one you choose to build. This three-sided box is easy to assemble and easy to display on wall, shelf, or table top. If you do not have power tools at home, you should have the lumber yard cut the pieces for you.

If you are using ¼-inch plywood, cut a bottom piece 24 inches wide by 12 inches deep, cut two side pieces 12¼ inches wide by 11¼ inches high. The back should also be 24 inches wide by 11¼ inches high. The pieces should be laid out as shown to make sure you have them in the correct order. When folded up, the 11¼-inch edges of the back and sides should be next to one another. Glue and nail the back to the bottom piece, then both sides to the edges of the back and bottom. Let dry.

The plywood is the least expensive material, but for a little more, you could use a hardwood such as mahogany and have it planed down to ½-inch thickness. This would give you a more sturdy box. Don't forget to make size adjustments. The base would still be 24 inches wide by 12 inches deep, but now the sides would be 12½ inches wide and 11½ inches high. The back would be 24 inches wide and 11½ inches high. Assemble as before. If you live in a large city, you might be able to find hardwoods in the thinner sizes.

Basic Construction Layout

Decorated Shadow Box

To turn your three-sided box into a finished shadow box, start by painting the interior back and sides white. Apply a second coat. You may want to paper certain portions of the shops as we did. If you paper the whole shop (as in the millinery) you will not have to paint the walls first. Paint the floor and narrow edges dark brown. For the flooring, use Flexible Wood-Trim, which is real wood veneer and comes in one-inch rolls. You will need three rolls.

Cut the first roll into 11½-inch lengths. Cut these pieces into different widths, marking the pieces with a pencil and ruler on the reverse side for an even cut. To make it look even more like real flooring, cut each of these lengths once horizontally at random places, since most floor planks were not long enough to cover the length of the room. Glue the strips onto the box floor one at a time with Elmer's Contact Cement, leaving a small space between the "boards." Apply pressure for about a minute until dry and continue across the floor, cutting the second roll of veneer like the first. When you get to the third roll of veneer, make sure you leave a strip 24 inches long and ½ inch wide. This will be glued to the front of the vertical strips to finish off the room. When you have glued all the strips into place, apply two coats of varnish for a lasting, permanent finish.

Decorated Shadow Box

Shelf Unit

It would be hard to imagine a store without shelves. Merchandise would be scattered all over the floor or piled in heaps that could easily tumble. There would be little organization and it would be very difficult to find anything. Worst of all, the storekeeper could not use his space efficiently. It was probably for some or all of these reasons that shelves were invented.

For this unit, use ⅛-inch-thick basswood or balsa. Cut two end pieces 8⅜ inches long by 2¼ inches wide. Measure off 3 inches. At this point, cut into the width of the shelf and make the next 5⅜ inches only 1¼ inches wide. These will be for the top shelves. For the two shelves on the bottom level, cut two pieces 5¾ inches long by 2¼ inches wide. For the countertop, cut a piece 6 inches long and 2⅜ inches wide. Cut ⅛ inch from each side of this piece 1¼ inches long. (This will fit between the top unit with the counter overlapping the bottom shelves.) Cut three top shelves 5¾ inches long by 1¼ inches wide. For the top of the shelf unit, cut a piece 6 inches long by 1½ inches wide.

Shelf Unit

Mark the insides of the sides to show you where the shelves will go. The top shelves should have 1¼ inches between them (don't forget to allow for the ⅛-inch thickness), and the bottom ones should have 1⅜ inches between them. Using a clamp, glue the shelves into place, starting with the bottom three and working up. Stain and varnish when complete.

Long Counter

Counters served many purposes in small stores. They not only acted as storage units, but were also used as a barrier between the shopkeeper and the customer. The countertops held the scales and possibly the register. Items were displayed on their surfaces or wrapped for safekeeping when bought.

For this long counter, use wood that is ⅛ inch thick. Cut a piece 8 inches long by 2⅞ inches wide. This will be the front. Cut two sides

2 inches wide each by 2⅞ inches high. Glue a length of thick, square balsa wood behind the front of the counter at each end for a corner support. Glue the sides to the front, overlapping the front. Cut another piece of balsa wood 8½ inches wide by 2½ inches deep for the countertop. Round off the edges with sandpaper and glue to the top of the three-sided counter. Trim the front and sides of the counter as shown with ⅜-inch-wide balsa wood strips. Stain the counter and varnish.

Long Counter

Small Counter

For variety in your miniature store layout, you should have a small counter as well as a long one. Using ⅛-inch-thick wood, cut a front piece 6 inches long by 2⅞ inches high. Cut two sides 2 inches wide by 2⅞ inches high each. Make your countertop 6½ inches long by 2½ inches wide.

Use lengths of balsa wood glued behind the front of the counter as a brace and guide for gluing on the sides as you did with the long counter. Round off the countertop edges with sandpaper and glue on top of the three sides. Cover the front with ⅜-inch-wide strips of balsa wood. Trim the bottom and the bottom of the sides with ¼-inch-wide balsa strips. Stain and varnish.

Small Counter

Showcase

A showcase is a special display unit. It is a see-through counter. It lets the customer see merchandise as he would on a shelf but it keeps the items dust free while showing them off to their best advantage. These units were often used for baked goods in a sweet shop or general store. They could also hold a more valuable line of merchandise such as silverware or pewter in a general store, small toys in a toy shop, and specialty items such as fans and gloves in a millinery.

To make a showcase, cut two sides of ⅛-inch-thick wood 2 inches by 2⅞ inches each. For the base panel on the front, cut a piece 6 inches long by ⅝ inch wide. For the top panel, cut a piece 6 inches long by ⅜ inch wide. The two end pieces should be 1⅞ inches long by ¼ inch wide. For the countertop, cut a piece 6½ inches long by 2½ inches wide. Since you can see through the front of a showcase, you should also have two shelves, each 5½ inches long by 2 inches wide.

Using a clamp, glue the two shelves between the sides, making sure that the lower shelf will be lower than the top of the base panel. When dry, stain and varnish this much. Next, cut a piece of clear acetate 5⅞ inches wide by 2½ inches wide and glue onto the edges of the side pieces. When dry, glue the bottom front panel into place, then the top, and finally the front sides. Round off the edges of the countertop with sandpaper and glue into place. Varnish and stain the remainder pieces.

Showcase

Ladder

Ladder

Every store needs a ladder. No shopkeeper is tall enough to reach the top shelf where those rarely sought items are stored. It might be a supplemental jar of candies in the sweet shop or an extra bolt of cloth in the general store, but sooner or later, there will be a need for these items and the shopkeeper will need help in reaching them.

For the sides of the ladder, cut two pieces of ⅛-inch-square balsa wood into 8-inch lengths. For the seven rungs, cut pieces of ⅛ inch doweling into the following lengths: bottom rung 1½ inches, 1 6/16 inches, 1 5/16 inches, 1 4/16 inches, 1 3/16 inches, 1 2/16 inches, and finally the top rung should be 1 1/16 inches wide. Glue the rungs between the sides, approximately one inch apart and put between a clamp (two heavy books will also work if you don't have a clamp) until dry. Varnish.

Cash Register

Who can imagine a shop without a cash register? There were some in the early eighteen hundreds before the cash register was invented in 1879. Before then, stores had a slot in the top of the counter and money would fall into a drawer beneath it. But for our purposes, the shops will be late eighteenth century with a cash register for storing money.

Start with a piece of quarter round ⅝ inch in diameter. Cut a piece 1¼ inches long. For the base, cut a 1¼-inch-long piece of balsa wood that is ½ inch thick by 1 inch wide. Glue the quarter round to the top of this piece, matching the backs so that the bottom piece overlaps to form a drawer. For the back of the register, use ⅛-inch-thick balsa and cut a piece 1¼ inches wide by 1⅝ inches high. Glue to the back of the base and quarter round. Stain and varnish the register. For the keys, pound nine small brass nails into the quarter round as shown. Use one nail in the middle of the base for the drawer pull. For the crank, hammer a nail into a reverse S shape and push into the right side of the quarter round.

Wall Clock

Every store needs a clock. It tells the shopkeeper when to open and when to close. It tells the customer whether he can browse or

Cash Register

Wall Clock

whether he must buy immediately in order to make another appointment. Everyone concerned with time watches it tick away the minutes that become hours and then days in the life of a store.

For our clock, use ⅛-inch-thick balsa wood. Start the clock face with a square measuring 1¼ inches square. Mark 6/16 inch from each end all the way around, leaving ½ inch (8/16) in the middle of each of the four sides. Using the 6/16-inch measurement, cut a triangle from each corner as shown in the following drawing:

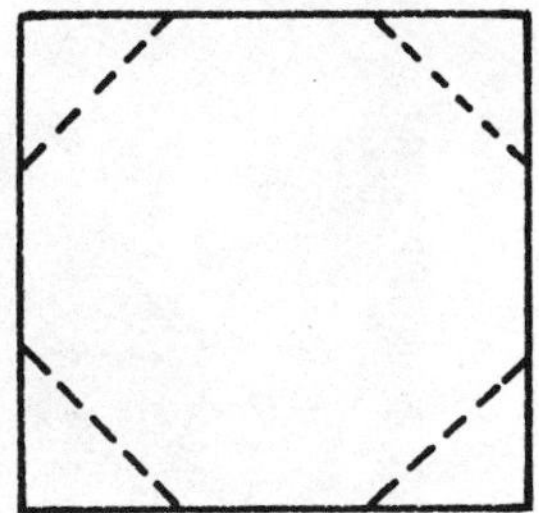

You now have an eight-sided figure that is approximately ½ inch on each side.

For the base, cut a piece of the same size balsa wood 2 inches long by ¾ inch wide. Glue this to the bottom of the octagonal shape starting ¼ inch from the top. For the pendulum cover, cut a piece of the same balsa ½ inch square. Round off the bottom with sandpaper and glue onto the base as shown. Stain and varnish. For the clock face, find an appropriate size and shape in a magazine and glue into place.

Wall Telephone

Alexander Graham Bell got the patent for the first telephone in 1876. Within ten years the Bell Telephone System was formed, but home telephones were still rare. It was not unusual to find the telephone in the general store the only one in a small town.

For this early model, start with a strip of balsa wood that is 1 inch wide and ½ inch thick. Cut a piece to a length of 1½ inches. For the back of the telephone, use ⅛-inch-thick wood and cut a piece 2¼ inches high and 1¼ inches wide. Glue the thick piece on top of this one and round off the top edge of the back piece. Stain and varnish.

Stick a black pushpin into the bottom lower half of the telephone for the mouthpiece. For the bells, use two small half beads. Paint them a brass color and glue into place as shown. Bend a nail into a reverse S shape and push into the right side of the telephone for the crank.

Telephone

For the earpiece, use another black pushpin. Cut a length of heavy thread 3½ inches long. To attach to the pushpin, cut out a cardboard circle the size of the smaller edge of the pushpin. Using a needle, put the thread through the center of this piece of cardboard, remove the needle and knot the thread. Remove the pin from the pushpin and glue the cardboard holding the thread to the smaller edge. Paint the cardboard black. Using the needle again, push the other end of the thread through the back of the telephone and knot again. For the hook, fold a piece of thin wire into a T shape about ½ inch tall. Fold the end of the T up into a U shape. Push the bottom of the T into the upper left side of the telephone with a touch of glue. Hang the earpiece in place and your shopkeeper is ready to ring.

Door

A door adds dimension to any shop by making the viewer think there is something beyond. In the general store, the door may lead to a butchering area or a storage room. In the schoolhouse, the door became the front entrance. In the confectionery, it might lead to a bakery or a back entrance. As shop creator, the choice is yours.

For a door, use ⅛-inch-thick wood. Cut a door 3 inches wide and 6¾ inches high. For the door frame, use ³/₁₆-inch-thick wood that is ¼ inch wide. Cut two side pieces 6¾ inches long and one top piece 3½ inches long. Glue around the door, overlapping the top piece on the sides. For the trim on the door, use ⅛-inch-thick strips that are ⅜ inch wide. Cut two strips, each 6 inches long and two strips, each 3 inches long. Glue the two short strips onto the top and bottom of the door, then the sides between them. For the middle piece, cut another piece of the ⅜-inch-wide strip to a length of 2¼ inches. Glue into place. Cut two more pieces into 2¾ inch lengths and glue between the middle and the top and bottom of the door as shown. Stain and varnish. Metal doorknobs are available from dealers.

Door

2

General Store

General stores played a major role in the life of every small community around the turn of the century. Often located at a major crossroad, the general store was more than the only merchandising outlet available to the citizens. The important events in a person's life either happened there or were reported there. Births were announced with an order for nipples and news of a death came when someone ordered hinges for a casket. If a man wanted to cuss the government or debate the Bible, he usually did it at the general store. Since the store also held the post office, major news items reported in letters were quickly made common knowledge. Like many other such establishments, the Cilley General Store in Plymouth Notch, Vermont, had the only telephone. As late as 1923, Vice-President Calvin Coolidge, a native of the town, would use it to call Washington for news.

Although weekend trade was hectic, the weekdays were often slow. Bad weather would also find local farmers gathered around the pot-bellied stove chewing tobacco and debating fence laws and politics. Somc would pitch dollars, others preferred to play checkers. All liked to talk.

As the center of commerce for the community, the general store carried an amazing variety of items. There was fresh produce, much of which came from the farmers themselves in trade for goods, and barreled goods like coffee, molasses, whiskey, vinegar, and lard. Canned goods sat next to bottles of castor oil and boxes of crackers along the shelves and there was always a large supply of cigars and

General Store

chewing tobacco along with the penny candy. There were shelves of commercial medicines as well as the folk remedies of the day. Sewing notions and materials were in abundance as were other household necessities such as cooking pots, oil lamps, and curios of every description. School children stocked up on slates and pencils and even their primers, while farmers outfitted their mules and took stock of their tools at the beginning of every new season. Ready-made clothes were available for special occasions along with factory-made shoes. For reading, there was always the Bible or the *Farmer's Almanac.*

Most of the orders came to the merchant on slips of paper carried by a young child. Business was good as long as the customer's credit held out, and the merchant kept a close watch on his customer's crops to see how much credit he could allow toward the harvest.

For the miniature store in this chapter, you will need the basic box, three shelf units, a long counter, a short counter, and a display showcase. You will also need the ladder, cash register, clock, and telephone. Most of the other items in the photograph are pictured with instructions in the following chapter. It was impossible to reproduce the pewter, glass, and woven items, and these were purchased, along with the rocker and boots, to fill out the shelves.

In making the items for the general store, remember to make more than one, since a storekeeper would normally have several to choose from. On such a small scale, two or three items give the illusion of quantity.

The directions for some of the items on the shelves such as the toys and school supplies will be found in the chapters dealing with the toy shop and one-room schoolhouse.

Finally, you might have noticed that we did not leave the walls of the shadow box white. We tried this at first, but the store simply did not look old. We got the effect we wanted by covering the walls of our general store with a walnut grained contact paper. By measuring the pieces first, we simply laid them in place, being careful to match the corners.

Pot-Bellied Stove

A pot-bellied stove was part of the necessary equipment of every general store during the late 1800s. It was used for far more than just heating the building. Customers would pull up benches and kegs and gather around the stove to spin yarns and whittle away their time. They played checkers or cards and spat their tobacco juices around the base of the stove. Since it played such an important role in the full-sized stores, no miniature store should be without one.

To make a miniature stove, use an unfinished acorn shape from shelving assemblies that are found in most hardware departments and unfinished furniture stores. Next, use ½-inch-thick balsa wood and cut a base 2 inches wide by 1⅝ inches deep. Gouge a round circle halfway through the middle of the piece and glue the acorn shape, top down, into that circle. For the top of the stove and the two doors, use ⅛ inch balsa wood. For the top, cut a circle 1½ inches in diameter and glue into place. For the bottom door, cut a piece 1⅝ inches long by ¼ inch wide. Glue to the front of the base. For the top door, cut a piece ¾ inch wide by ½ inch high. To get a perfect fit, hold a piece of sandpaper face up on the curve of the stove and rub this piece of balsa on it until it takes the curve of the stove. Remove the sandpaper and glue into place. Use ½-inch doweling for the feet and the stove pipe. Cut four pieces, each ¼ inch thick, for the feet. Glue into place. For the pipe, cut a piece 5¼ inches long. At the 3-inch point, cut the piece in half on the diagonal. Turn the small piece upside down and glue together to form the joint. Glue the pipe, long piece down, to the top of the stove. For the wall shield, cut a piece of cardboard, using a quarter as a pattern, and glue to the end of the stovepipe. Paint the entire stove black and nail two small brass nails on the doors for handles.

Pot-Bellied Stove

Woodbox

Woodbox

Pot-bellied stoves needed constant refurbishing, and a woodbox was often found nearby filled with a good supply of wood. For this box, use ⅛-inch-thick balsa wood or basswood. Cut a base 2 inches by 2¼ inches. For the front, cut a piece 2 inches wide by ⅞ inch high. Cut a back piece 2 inches wide by 1¾ inches high. Cut two side pieces, each 2⅛ inches wide. The tops should be cut on a slant starting at ⅞ inch and graduating to 1¾ inches. Glue the four sides together, overlapping the front and back, and glue this piece to the base. Stain and varnish. For pieces of wood, cut twigs broken into small pieces.

Scales

Much of the produce was fresh in the general store. Most of it came in on a trade for other items from the local farmers, and scales were needed to determine the price per pound. The personality of the shopkeeper often determined if the scales read a half ounce over or under.

For our scales, you will need two deep-centered buttons, preferably brass. Look in the loose button box in your local fabric store. You might find these buttons camouflaged as the rims of buttons with fancy interiors. Simply pry the middle part out of the button and paint gold. For the base you will need ⅛-inch-thick balsa wood. Cut a piece 1 inch by 1⅜ inches. Make a ledge for the weights by trimming the sides of the front until you have a center piece left that measures ½ inch wide by ⅜ inch deep. Next, use ¼-inch-thick balsa and cut a piece 1⅜ inches long by ⅝ inch wide. Glue to the top of the first piece, leaving the weight ledge in the front. Round off the top edge of the new piece with sandpaper. Next, use the ¼-inch-thick balsa as the width and cut a piece ⅝ inch wide. Round off the top again and glue to the middle of the base. To hold the buttons, use a 3/16-inch-wide strip of balsa cut to a length of 1⅜ inches. Glue the buttons to each end and glue onto the base as shown. A single nail may be used in the middle to secure it. Use three different-sized dowels for the weights and glue small pieces to the front of the scales. Paint these gold and the rest of the scales black.

Scales

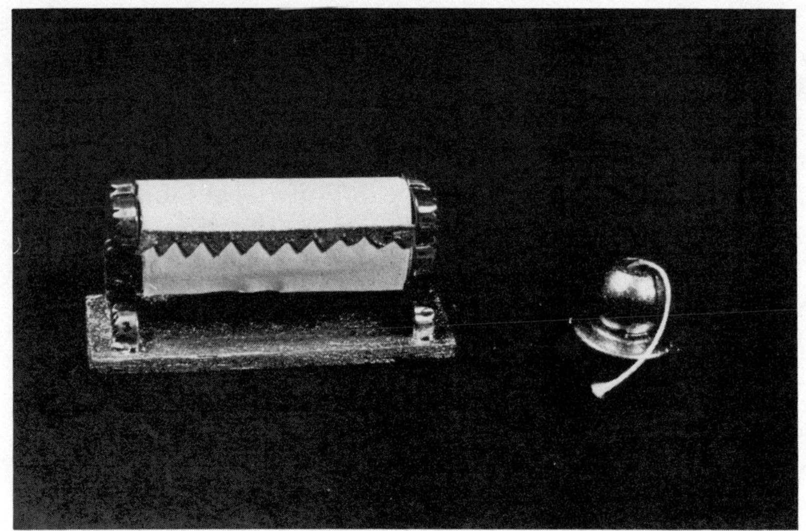

Paper Cutter and String Holder

Butcher Block

Paper Cutter and String Holder

Although paper bags had been invented in the latter part of the 1800s, they did not gain popularity immediately, and packages were still being wrapped with paper and string. For the paper cutter, start with ⅛-inch-thick balsa and cut a base piece 1¾ inches long by ⅝ inch wide. Paint gold. For the roll, use a ½ inch diameter dowel and cut to a length of 1¼ inches. Glue a strip of white paper to this dowel, leaving the end to hang down. Find two buttons similar in shape to the ones shown and glue the roll between them. Glue the buttons onto the base. For the cutter, cut a jagged strip of cardboard, paint gold, and glue into place.

For the string holder, find a small bead and glue to a flat button for a base. Paint both gold. Glue a small piece of string into the top of the bead and let it hang over the side.

Butcher Block

The general store proprietor was many things including a butcher. Cooling meat might be stored in the back while salted meat often hung from rafters. Although he could buy the slaughtered meat from local farmers, he would have to cut it into the desired sizes for the customers. The storekeeper would be forced to do more of this if his store was located in a small town than if it was situated at a crossroad in the country where most of the customers did their own butchering.

For this butcher block, use ⅛-inch-thick basswood. Cut two sides, each 1¾ inches long by 1¼ inches wide. Cut a front and back piece, each 2½ inches long and 1¼ inches wide. Bevel the narrow edges and glue together as shown. Cut another piece 2¼ inches long by 1¼ inches wide. Cut strips 2¼ inches long and 3/32 inch wide and glue across this whole piece. When dry, glue this piece between the four sides so that it is even with the top. Using ¼-inch-diameter dowels, cut four legs, each 2½ inches long. Carve with sandpaper as shown and glue into the four corners beneath the block. For the piece that holds the tools, cut two pieces of the ⅛-inch basswood 2 inches long and ¼ inch wide. Cut six small ¼-inch squares. Glue the first long piece to the left front of the block. Glue the six small squares onto this, leaving varied spaces between them. Glue the other long piece on top and smooth the two sides with sandpaper. Varnish the butcher block. For the tools, use balsa wood and sand them into shape, making the knife and cleaver 1¼ inches long and the tenderizer 1 inch long. Paint black and silver.

Mailbox

Mailbox

The general store often doubled as a post office in small communities. Packages, newspapers, letters—all came into the general store where members of the community could claim their mail. It was here, too, that packages and letters were mailed and stamps were sold.

For this wall unit, use 3/16-inch-thick balsa wood for the shelves. Make them all 1 inch wide. Cut three 4½-inch lengths and two 2½-inch lengths. Using ⅜-inch-wide strips of balsa wood, cut twenty pieces, each 1 inch long. Starting with the shorter shelves, glue five of the strips along the top of each shelf, leaving ⅜ inch between them. Turn the shelf over and do the same on the other side of the shelf. Glue these shelves between the long ones, so that you have the letter slots on the left hand side and the shelves for packages on the right. Using ⅛-inch balsa wood, cut two end pieces 1 inch wide by 2 inches high and glue into place. Cut another piece of the ⅜-inch strip into a 2¼-inch length for the top of the unit. Write "U.S. Mail" on this strip, glue into place as shown and stain everything. Make tiny envelopes with colored stamps for the slots and cover pieces of balsa wood with brown wrapping paper and tie with string for the packages. Addresses and stamps may be drawn on with felt-tipped pens.

Storekeepers needed a place to write orders, tabulate bills, and store the hundreds of slips of paper that orders were written on until they could be recorded in an account book. A countertop desk served their purpose without taking as much room as a full-sized desk.

Use ⅛-inch-thick basswood or balsa wood for this piece. Cut a base piece 2½ inches long by 2¼ inches wide (length across front). Cut a piece 1¾ inches wide by ½ inch high for the back. Cut a piece 1¾ inches wide and ¼ inch high for the front. Cut two pieces for the sides, which will be 2³/₁₆ inches across at the bottom, ½ inch tall on one side, and ¼ inch on the other. Start to slant your cut ¹¹/₁₆ of an inch from the side that is ½ inch high, like this:

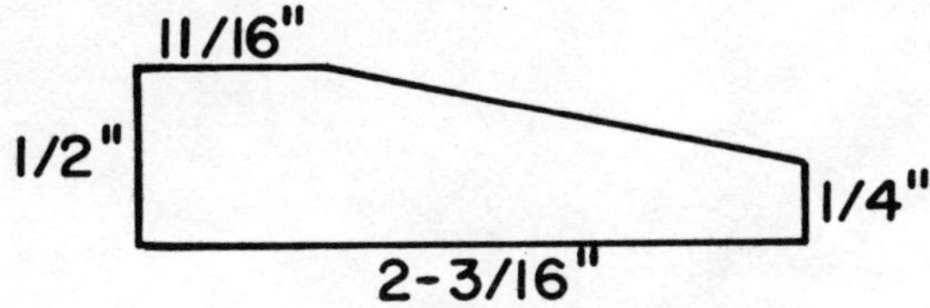

For the top of the desk, cut a piece 2¼ inches long by ¹¹/₁₆ inch wide. The writing part of the desk should be 2¼ inches by 1⅝ inches. For the top, you will need 10 pieces of toothpicks or thin doweling cut to ¼-inch lengths. Onto these you will glue a U-shaped piece of wood 2 inches long by ⅜ inch wide, with each of the ends measuring ½ inch long.

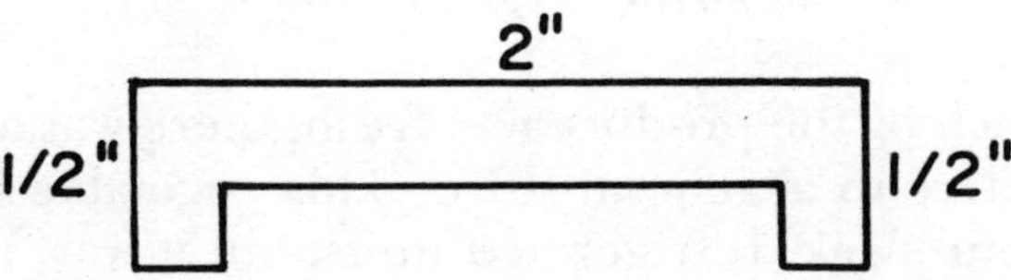

Glue the sides, front, and back pieces together, overlapping the sides. Glue this piece onto the base, making sure the backs are even. Glue the toothpicks onto the smaller piece of the top of the desk, topping it off with the U shape. (If you would like something sturdier, you might want to drill holes partway into the pieces for the toothpicks to fit into, and in this case you should use toothpicks ⅜ inch in length.) Glue this piece onto the back and sides of the desk and finish by gluing a piece of material under this piece and under the writing part of the desk so that it may be lifted. Stain and varnish.

Countertop Desk

Countertop Vegetable Bin

Since so much of the produce was fresh, there was a great need for layout counters in a general store. This vegetable bin was the forerunner of our sleek, refrigerated units, but it was, in fact, little more than a wooden holder. For the base, use either ⅛-inch-thick balsa or basswood and cut a piece 1⅜ inches wide by 4 inches long. For the front and back, cut pieces 4 inches long by ⅜ inch wide. For the sides and dividers, cut five pieces, each 1⅛ inch wide by ⅜ inch high. Glue the sides to the front and back, overlapping the front and back. Glue the dividers into place, leaving approximately 6/8 of an inch between each one.

For the vegetables, use bread dough or Repla-Cotta, painting them with acrylic paints in the appropriate colors. The signs were made on small pieces of white cardboard glued to pieces of toothpicks.

Countertop Vegetable Bin

Egg and Berry Baskets

A large part of the general store business lay in trading. The local farmers would bring their fresh produce and trade for factory-made items. There would be berries and fresh vegetables from the garden in season and eggs on a more regular basis.

For the egg basket, use a small, woven basket, which may be found in toy stores or novelty shops. Make three dozen eggs from Repla-Cotta, bake, paint white, and glue into place.

For the berry basket, use 1/32-inch-thick balsa wood. Cut into 3/8-inch-wide strips. Cut two pieces into 1½-inch lengths. Soak the pieces until they are pliable. Measure into ½-inch sections. Bend both pieces into a U shape of ½-inch sections. When dry, glue one middle on top of another. Cut another piece of the 1/32-inch-thick balsa into a strip 1/8 inch wide and 2¼ inches long. Soak this, too, and bend into a shape to fit around the top of the box. When dry, glue into place. Cut off any excess from the sides and fill the berry basket with Repla-Cotta berries baked and painted red or blue for blueberries. Make several for the countertop.

Egg and Berry Baskets

Wooden Barrel and Checkerboard

Wooden barrels were staples in country stores. They not only held many items of merchandise, but they were also used as impromptu seats and often held the popular checkerboard when a game started around the stove. They came in many sizes and you should have several scattered around the store.

This barrel (and the others) started from blocks of balsa wood. Using an X-acto knife, cut a square 1½ inches square by 1¾ inches high. Slice off the square edges and sand until you have a rounded barrel shape, wider in the middle and smaller on the top and bottom. Stain when finished and add thin strips of black cloth tape for the bands.

For the checkerboard, cut a picture of one from a Christmas toy catalog (or any magazine), glue to a piece of cardboard, and glue to the top of the barrel.

Flour and Sugar Sacks

Flour and sugar were bought in volume during the late 1800s because women did most of their own baking. The sacks were cloth instead of paper like today, and they were usually kept off floor level because of the rats.

For the flour sack, use white cotton material. Cut a piece 4 inches long by 1½ inches wide. Turn to the wrong side. Fold in half and sew up the sides, using a ¼-inch seam. Turn back to the right side and make a circular design with a red waterproof pen, using a nickel for the circle pattern. Use either your own name, or a popular name such as Pillsbury. Fill with sugar and close the top with a handstitch, leaving the two ends longer for handling.

Wooden Barrel and Checkerboard

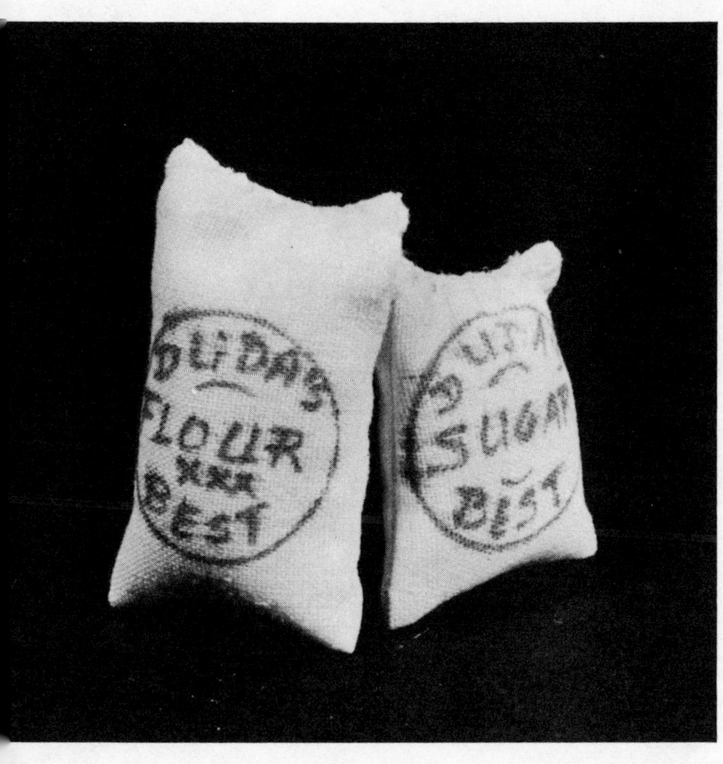

Flour and Sugar Sacks

Make the sugar sacks the same way, but start with a smaller piece of white cotton. Make this piece 3 inches long by 1½ inches wide. Fold and sew together as before and make a similar pattern on the front, replacing the word *flour* with *sugar*. Fill with sugar and close as before.

Crates

Modern merchandising methods had not been invented during the early days of the general store, and produce was simply displayed in the crates it came in. The customer often chose his own and had to if the storekeeper was involved in a game of checkers.

These crates may be made from either ⅛-inch-thick basswood or balsa wood.

For the apple crate, cut a base 2½ inches long by 1¼ inches wide. Cut two sides, each 2¼ inches long by 1¼ inches wide. Cut two end pieces and one middle piece 1 inch wide by 1¼ inches high. Glue the four ends together, overlapping the sides on the ends. Glue the middle divider into place. When dry, glue onto the base and varnish.

For the potato crate, use ¼-inch-wide balsa wood or cut basswood to this width. Cut 8 pieces, each 2 inches long for the sides.

Crates

Cut 8 pieces, each 1 inch long for the ends. Cut three pieces, each 2¼ inches long for the bottom and four pieces, each 1¼ inches long for the inner guards. Glue four side pieces onto two of the inner guards. Do the same with the other four. Glue the shorter end pieces over these sides, matching the corners. Turn the box over and glue the three bottom pieces across the top. Varnish, turn over, and fill with potatoes.

For the orange crate, you will need four ½-inch-wide by 2¼-inch long pieces for the sides. Then cut two end and one middle piece, 1 inch wide by 1¼ inches high. For the bottom, you'll need two pieces, each 2¼ inches long by ⅜ inch wide, and three cross pieces, ⅛ inch wide by 1¼ inches long. Glue the sides to the two end pieces, overlapping the sides and matching tops and bottoms but leaving a space in the middle. Glue the middle partition into place. For the bottom of the box, glue the two lengths into place, making them even with the sides, and, finally, glue the cross pieces over the ends and in the middle to keep the produce off the floor. Varnish.

For the fruit, you may use homemade bread dough or Repla-Cotta.

Boxes and Cans of Food

Who can imagine a country store without shelves of food in boxes and cans? Although much of the food was homegrown and canned or smoked, there were always delicacies and staples for times when people ran out of their own stock.

For the boxes of food, use pieces of 3/16-inch-thick balsa wood cut into various sizes and painted appropriate colors. Then decorate these pieces or cover them with strips of paper depicting product names and designs. Gluing several of the same-shaped boxes together (only the front one needs a label) keeps the boxes from falling over and makes the shelves look as if they are well stocked.

For the cans of food, use ⅜-inch-thick dowels. Cut into ⅜-inch and ½-inch lengths and paint silver. Cover with paper strips cut to fit around the can. Draw labels with fine-tipped felt pens. You may use standard names or make up your own. When the designs are dry, glue the strips to the cans and pile in rows on your shelves.

Boxes and Cans of Food

Jars of Candy

Weekends usually brought the rural families to the general store and the children would beg for candy treats much as they do today. These candy jars were made from plastic tubing found in hardware stores. Cut pieces ¾ inch and ⅞ inch long. Use black matting board for the tops and bottoms, cutting circles to fit the ends. Glue the bottoms into place. For the individual candies, use cocoanut petites, sugar crystals, and nonpareils found in the cooking section of the grocery store. The sticks of candy are made by nailing two nails into a board about 18 inches apart. Tie two pieces of heavy string or thin yarn to one nail, twist together, and tie to the other nail. Cover the thread with diluted glue and leave overnight. By morning you'll be ready to cut your candy sticks to size. For the tops of the containers, use another circle of the black matting board and glue into place. Top with a dab of glue and a crystal bead.

Bolts of Cloth and Spools of Thread

Fabrics played a major role in a person's life around the turn of the century. An order for birdseye announced the birth of a new child in a household, while an order for shroud material brought news of a death. In between there were orders for calicos and ginghams, paisleys and denims, orders for go-to-meeting-type material and school-type material, maternity dress fabric and party dress fabric.

Jars of Candy

Bolts of Cloth and Spools of Thread

With so many possibilities, the general store keeper kept a large stock of material on hand.

For a selection in the miniature store, start with a piece of thick cardboard 1 inch wide by 2 inches long. Find pieces of material with tiny prints (friends who sew can be helpful in this area) and cut pieces 12 inches long by 4 inches wide. Press the material in half lengthwise and fold around the piece of cardboard. Tack with a couple of stitches at the top to keep in place.

Spools of thread will be needed to sew the garments, and for these, you will need a dowel strip ⅛ inch in diameter. Cut the dowel into ⅜-inch pieces. For the ends, cut holes with a paper punch from a sheet of white cardboard. Glue to the ends of the dowel and draw a hole in the middle with a pen. Coat the dowel with glue and wind thread onto it, using a touch of glue to secure the end when you feel you have enough.

Lace, Yarn, and Bias Tape

The Victorian era called for fancy trims. Carpenters put gingerbread and scrollwork on their houses and women put lots of lace trimmings and bindings on their dresses. Lace and bias tapes were, therefore, necessities as were the skeins of yarn. Yarn was needed for knitting sweaters and winter hats with matching scarves, not to mention the oft-lost mittens.

Miniature laces may be found in many places. The edges of old laces will often yield a row of lace, or ask a friend or relative to crochet a tiny length. Wind these pieces of lace around pieces of red cardboard that measure ½ inch wide by 1 inch high. Secure the end with a dab of glue.

The bias tape is a thin piece of material wound and glued around a piece of white cardboard ½ inch long by ¼ inch wide. Cut a ¼-inch-wide strip of white paper and glue around the middle, labeling as shown.

For the yarn, find the thinnest knitting yarn available and wind around a 1-inch piece of cardboard about ten times. Remove from the cardboard, keeping the skein shape, and fasten with a strip of paper ⅜ inch wide by 1 inch long. Glue the end in place and make several skeins in different colors for the shelves.

Wooden Washtub and Board

In the late 1800s, women were still doing the laundry by hand, removing dirt and grime with the help of a scrubbing board. They washed less often and children were taught to be more careful, since they only had two or three changes of clothing.

For this miniature wooden washtub, start with the bottom of a 2½-inch-in-diameter unfinished pillbox. Cut off the inner rim and

Lace, Yarn, and Bias Tape

Wooden Washtub and Board

stain. Use two staple nails for the handles and strips of gold paper for the rings around the outside.

The washboard is made from balsa wood. Use ¼-inch-wide strips for the top and sides. Cut two pieces, each 2 inches long, for the sides and sand one end of each to a point. Cut a piece 1¼ inches long for the top. For the middle, use ⅛-inch-thick balsa and cut a piece 1¼ inches long by ¾ inch wide. Score 1 inch of the top with an X-acto knife and ruler. At the top of the scoring, glue a ⅛-inch-thick strip of balsa wood cut to a length of ¾ inch. Paint the scored part of the wood silver. When dry, glue this piece between the side strips you made before and add the top. Stain and varnish everything but the silver part.

Books

In many areas of the country, the general store was also the public library and book distributor. Teachers ordered texts and preachers ordered Bibles. Account books were bought for keeping farm records, and leather-bound photo albums were bought for parlor tables. The *Farmer's Almanac* was a popular item as was the McGuffey reader.

For the Bible and photo album, start with ¼ inch balsa wood. Cut pieces 1 inch long by ¾ inch wide. Paint the edges gold. Cut pieces of leather or suede or possibly velveteen 1 inch wide by 2 inches long. Glue around the outside of the book and label with pieces of construction paper. For the photo album, cut a strip ⅛ inch wide by ¾ inch long and glue to the side as shown. Use a small, brass nail for the lock.

Account books and other simpler items may be made with thinner pieces of balsa wood and painted gold around the rim and various colors on the cover. Label as before.

Lamps and Candles

Kerosene lamps were not immediately accepted because the pine plank houses of the late 1800s burned so quickly. The lamps were thought to explode, and women continued to hand dip their candles for many years after the advent of the kerosene lamp.

This *Gone with the Wind* lamp started with two wooden beads about ¾ inch in diameter. Paint them white. Flatten a small ball of Play-Doh and glue between the beads for the middle. Insert the edge of a screw type earring into the Play-Doh for the adjuster on the lamp. Glue a

Books

Lamps and Candles

gold bead cap to the bottom of one bead for the base and a crystal bead to the top. Paint flowers on the front of the globes and paint the band across the middle gold.

For the hand-dipped candles, use the leftover ends of regular white candles. Cut six pieces of kite string (or any thin, white string) into 5-inch lengths. Melt the candle leftovers in a small pan. When the wax has completely melted, remove the pan from the stove. Holding the middle of a piece of string, dip each end of the string into the liquid. Continue until you have twelve candles. Make the candles about 1 inch in length. If the wax in the pan starts to harden before you are finished, simply reheat. Hang the string over a coat hanger until the candles are dry. Then cut the string and stack the candles. The box is made from ⅛-inch-thick balsa wood. For the base, cut a piece 1¼ inches long by ⅝ inch wide. For the sides, use strips that are ⅜ inch wide. Cut two pieces each ⅞ inch long for the ends and two pieces each 1¼ inches long for the sides. Glue the sides together around the base. Stain and fill with the candles.

Iron and Carpet Beater

The general store was the forerunner of the modern department store and, as such, sold many of the housekeeping necessities of the day. In the late 1800s, before the advent of permanent-pressed clothes and linens, an iron had a prominent place in every household. Wall-to-wall carpeting had not come into vogue yet either, so every spring and fall would find area rugs slung over clotheslines as busy housewives attempted to remove the dust with a carpet beater.

For the miniature iron, start with ⅛-inch-thick balsa wood. Cut a piece ¾ inch long by ½ inch wide. Sand the two long edges until they meet in a point. For the handle, use picture hanging wire. Cut a piece 1¼ inches in length. Fold into a U shape and press the two ends, coated with glue, into the soft balsa wood as shown. Paint the iron black.

For the carpet beater, start with a piece of picture-hanging wire 12 inches long. Start from one end and measure off 2½ inches. At this point, make a circle to the right, using 2 more inches. Fold the long end over the first part of the circle and make another 2-inch circle to the left. Make a final 3-inch circle through the center of both previous circles and twist the rest of the wire around the handle. Hang or store on the store shelves.

Banjo

Country entertainment may have been less sophisticated during the latter part of the last century, but it certainly was not lacking. There were quilting bees and political rallies and country fairs. One

Iron and Carpet Beater

of the most popular forms of entertainment was the barn dance, and musicians would often go to the country store to replace strings or buy a new banjo.

For the banjo, start with balsa wood 3/16 inch thick. Using a quarter, draw a circle for the banjo soundboard or belly. Cut a square around this circle and form the circle with sandpaper. Paint the edge black and the two sides white. For the top of the banjo, use ¼-inch-thick balsa and cut a piece 1½ inches long by ½ inch wide. Form the head and neck of the banjo with sandpaper and paint black. Cut a notch in the base of the neck and glue to the top of the soundboard. Insert two brad nails on either side of the head for the tuners and one in the top of the head to hold the string. Insert three nails next to one another in the middle of the soundboard. Tie heavy-duty string around the single nail in the head and string around each of the nails in the soundboard, always bringing it back to

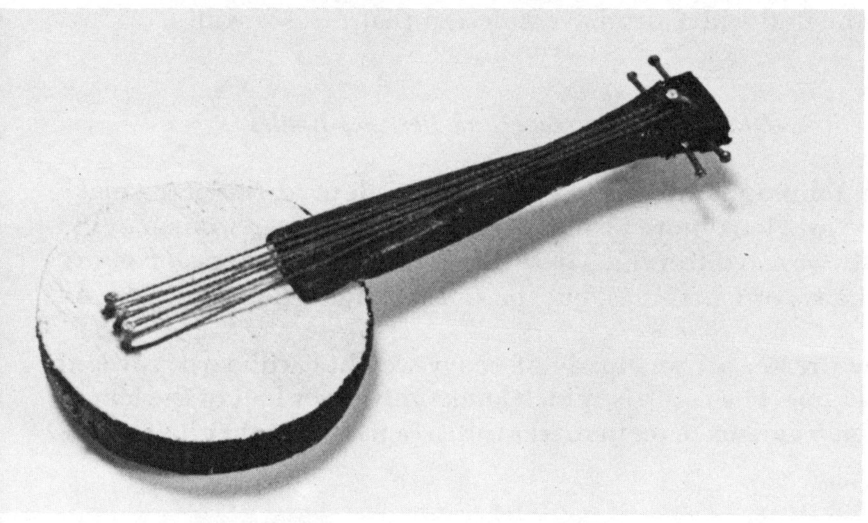

Banjo

pass over the one in the head. Pull taut and tie the end around the nail in the head and you're ready to pluck.

You can make guitars the same way by changing the shape of the soundboard.

Vegetable Cutter, Cookie Cutters, and Bread Pan

Women have always enjoyed anything that helps them in the kitchen. Fancy cookies were easily made with cookie cutters such as these, and bread would rise to a conventional shape if left in a pan such as this. Cole slaw and other dishes requiring grated vegetables were quickly made with a grater. For all of these items, you will need heavy-weight aluminum foil found in hobby shops.

For the vegetable grater, cut a piece ¾ inch wide by 1¼ inches long, leaving a thin strip 1 inch long on one side, ½ inch from the end. Turn over the piece of foil. Using the point of a pencil, punch numerous small holes beneath and to the right of the thin strip. With the help of a pencil, fold the foil into the shape of a grater, rounding it in the front, but flattening the edges together in the back. Fold the extra strip into the shape of a handle and your grater is finished.

For the bread pan, start with a piece of foil 1¾ inches long by 1 inch wide. Working along the shorter edges, make a ¼-inch slit ¼ inch from each end. Make ¼-inch folds all the way around the pan. These will be the sides. Fold the long sides up first and then fold the tips, which you have cut, in toward one another. Now fold the short ends of the pan up to cover these ends and you have a bread pan.

The cookie cutters are made from ⅛-inch-wide foil cut to various lengths. The heart, for example, was made from a piece 2 inches long. Experiment with different lengths for different shapes and simply cut off the end when you have a design that pleases you.

Dresser Set, Necklace, and Perfume Bottles

For thousands of years, women have desired things to make them feel and look more beautiful, and the small town woman of the late 1800s was no different. These things were special-occasion items, for birthdays or Christmas, but the smart shopkeeper kept them on hand.

The dresser set was made of heavy-weight cardboard, covered with gold foil. The comb is ¾ inch long. Only cover half of the length of the comb and make teeth marks with a pen on the other half. Make

Vegetable Cutter, Cookie Cutters, and Bread Pan

Dresser Set, Necklace, and Perfume Bottles

the brush 1 inch long and glue sparkles to the middle of the top. For the brush, cut a small circle of felt and glue to the bottom. The mirror should be 1¼ inches long. Cover the top with sparkles and glue a small circle of foil to the underside.

The necklace is a ring of small beads strung on a piece of string that was then tied. The Barbie doll pearl necklaces also work well in the showcase.

The perfume bottles were made from beads and bead caps. Use gold bead caps for the bottoms and glue different colored and different shaped crystal beads onto the bases. Top with a small dark bead.

Rope, Shovel, and Axe

Every spring would find farmers in the general store restocking their plowline ropes and tools. An axe was a year-round necessity and was used for clearing land in the summer and chopping wood for fireplaces in the winter. Shovels were always needed for removing earth, coal, or snow.

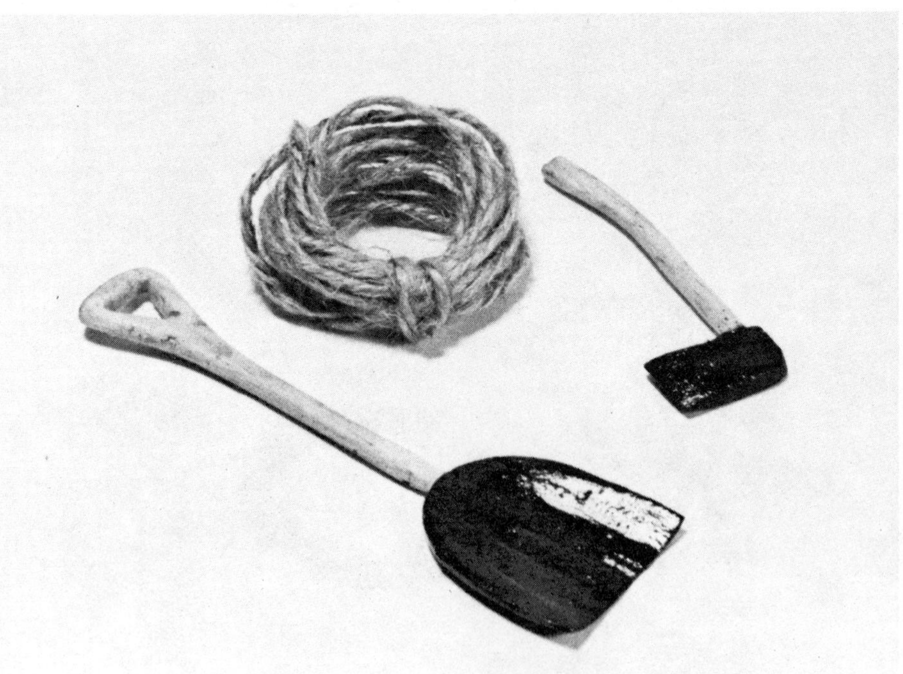

Rope, Shovel, and Axe

For the rope, use heavy-duty twine. Wrap it around two of your fingers thirteen times, tie the end in a knot, and cut off the rest. Hang on a nail in the store.

For the shovel, start with a piece of ⅛-inch-thick balsa wood. Cut a piece 1 inch by 1⅛ inches. Using the longer side as the height, round off the top of the shovel and sandpaper. Sand the top of the straight side, sanding first down the middle on the top, then along the sides on the bottom until the shovel seems indented. When finished, paint black. For the handle, cut a piece of balsa wood 2½ inches long by ½ inch wide. Sand into the shape of a handle as shown and varnish. Glue the handle to the shovel and hang from nails along the wall.

Using balsa wood again, cut a piece 1¾ inches long by ¼ inch wide. Sand into an axe handle as shown, curving the bottom slightly. Varnish. For the axe head, cut a piece ½ inch by ⅜ inch. Cut the longer edge at a slant as shown so that the cutting edge is wider than the rest. Sand the cutting edge so that it appears sharp. Paint black. When dry, glue the axe head to the handle.

Paper Bags and Brooms

General stores were starting to move away from wrapping packages by the late 1800s as paper bags slowly came into use. After all, it was much easier just to slip the merchandise into a bag without having to wrap it into a bundle and tie it for safekeeping. Brooms were stacked in piles for sale, but there was also one around for cleaning up the store after closing.

For the paper bag, use a regular brown paper bag and cut a piece 4 inches long by 2½ inches wide. Make ¾-inch slits along the right side of the length of the bag as shown:

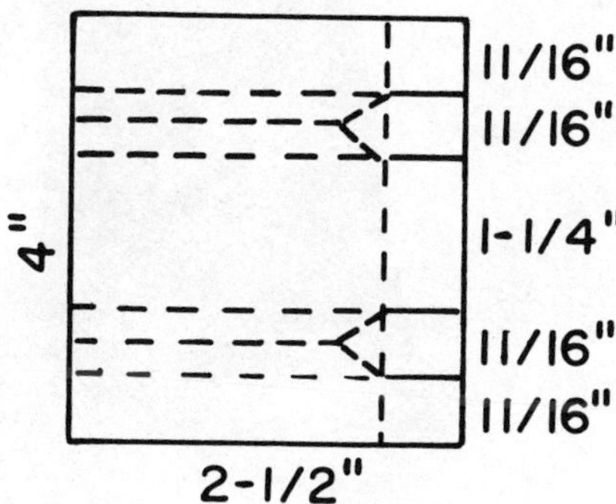

Fold the cut edges away from you. Then fold the rest of the bag. Starting at the top of the piece shown, fold away from you, then fold the middle toward you (these will be the sides), then away from you again in an accordian fold. Do the same for the bottom. Glue the two ends (the back of the bag) together. Form the bottom of the bag by folding and gluing the flaps together. Fold the sides under first. Cover this with the flap from the back, then all of these with the front flap.

The broom is made from a ¼-inch-diameter dowel cut to a length of 3 inches. Using straw cut to 2-inch lengths (ours were from an old broom), form the broom by tying these to the handle with heavy-duty thread. Make several to pile in a corner.

Paper Bags and Brooms

General stores were known for the variety of their lines. There were wooden things and glass things, ceramics and metals. There was also a whole line of goods that can be reproduced in miniature with copper wire.

If one was poor, he often bought his glasses "over the counter" in the general store. Using lightweight copper wire, twist several pairs for display in the fancy goods section of the store. Start with a small half circle. Continue in a straight line for about ¼ inch. Turn the wire to the right and make a circle for one eye, then cross over and make another circle. Turn the wire and take it back into another half circle to fit over the other ear and cut with wire cutters.

A potato masher was another convenience in every kitchen. For this one, start with the handle, making one about ½ inch long. Then bend the wire back and forth as shown, making four loops on one side and three on the other. Bend the wire back to the handle the same way you did for the other side and twist the end around the handle. Cover the handle with black tape (the kind you used on the barrel).

For the flyswatter, make a small loop with the wire and then make a handle 1¼ inches long. Form the wire into a square and twist the rest of the wire around the handle. For the swatter, you can use a small piece of pellon (a stiff lining) or part of an old piece of lace as we did here. Glue into place. When dry, cut away the excess material.

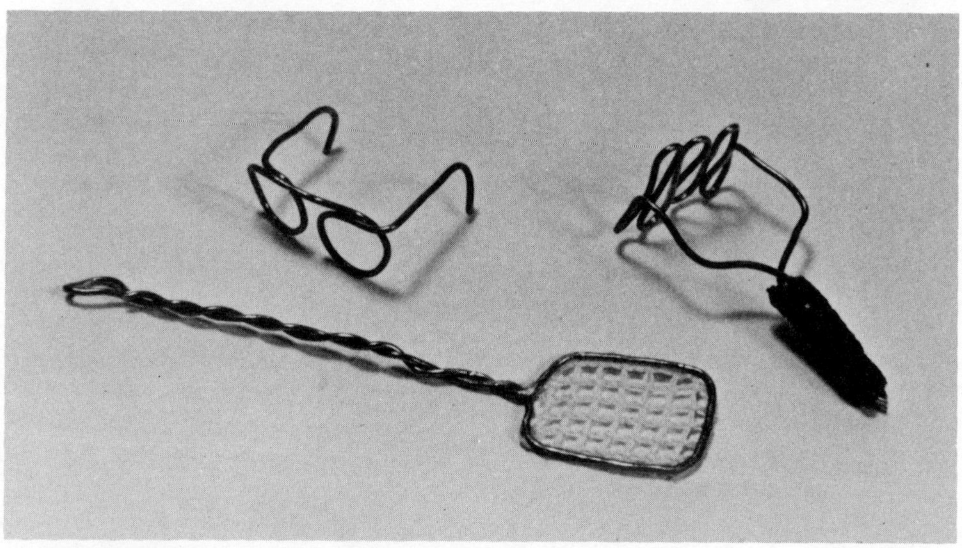

Glasses, Potato Masher, and Flyswatter

Ox Yoke

Spring planting time would always bring demands for outdoor tools of all kinds. New harnesses would be needed for the mules and new blades for the plows. The farmers who still plowed with oxen might need a new yoke for the team, and the general store proprietor was expected to have one on hand or be able to get one quickly.

For this ox yoke, use ¼-inch-thick balsa. Cut a piece 3 inches long and ¾ inch wide and sand into shape as shown. For the section that fits over the heads of the animals, use heavy wire cut to 2½-inch lengths. Bend as shown and push into the bottom of the yoke. Hang on the general store wall.

Ox Yoke

3

1899 Toy Shop

Toys have been providing amusement for children and adults since the time of the Pharaohs. Limestone toy animals with holes for pulling them were found in a Persian temple cornerstone dating back to 1100 years before Christ, and the Chinese were flying kites in 1000 B.C. Although many of the excavated toys, like rattles, were really ritual burial objects, many items were obviously toys, such as the balls and hobby horses, dolls, and animals on wheels. Homer mentions balls in 860 B.C. in the Odyssey, and it is well known that the children of Socrates had a hobbyhorse. Plato and Aristotle delighted in puppet shows, and the Greeks also had tops in 579 B.C. Tombs reveal that early Christian children were buried with their dolls, and balls are referred to in the Bible in Isaiah.

Toys developed with the civilizations, and during the Middle Ages great fairs were held on holidays and many "fairings" (toys) were sold by peddlers. Toys were in demand and toymakers formed guilds where they practiced their skills. The best toys found their way into the houses of royalty, but even the poorest children had simple toys to arouse their imaginations.

Toys became a part of life, and when the first English settlers came to America and landed at Roanoke Island, they brought toys with them. There is a record of one of the colonists giving an Indian child a doll as a sign of friendship almost 400 years ago. Unfortunately, the Roanoke colonists did not survive, and the Puritans who landed in Massachusetts had little tolerance for playthings. At a young age, the Puritan children learned to perform necessary labors in the household with little time left for pleasure. Christmas

Toy Shop

celebrations were not allowed, although children found time for games on Thanksgiving and election day celebrations. If the children had had more time for play and more toys to amuse them, we might have been spared the Salem witch trials in the 1690s where young girls let their imaginations run wild.

Unlike the stern English settlers, the new French, Spanish, and Dutch immigrants brought their holiday customs and their toys with them. The Dutch introduced St. Nicholas, their patron saint, who brought "fairings" for good children on December 6th. The German settlers in Pennsylvania brought their folk toys and the ability to make them. Toys were imported to meet the needs of the new settlers, and by the time of the Revolution, Christmas was a week-long celebration. During the war, American-made toys became scarce with other jobs to be done, but the British and Hessian soldiers brought their families and the children brought their toys, giving our craftsmen new ideas to develop after the war was over and things had settled down.

The greatest boost for the toy industry in America was the popularization of Santa Claus. Washington Irving told the story of the Dutch St. Nicholas in his *Knickerbocker History* in 1809, but it was Dr. Clement C. Moore who popularized the tradition. Dr. Moore, a biblical scholar, wrote "A Visit from St. Nicholas" in 1822 to amuse his children. Although he considered it poor writing, a friend had it published in the local newspaper and it became a permanent part of American Christmas celebrations. By the 1840s, Americans were exchanging Christmas cards and many families were decorating Christmas trees, a custom borrowed from the Germans.

By 1845, there was a toy shop in almost every town, and storekeepers from small towns went to New York to stock up for the Christmas holidays. Toy manufacturers sprang into existence around the country. Tin was used for pails, teapots, and pencil boxes. Ivory went into billiard balls, whistles, drum sticks, dominoes, and dice boxes. The first rubber factory started in 1811 and by 1850 was using rubber for balls, dolls' heads, and animals. China went into dolls' heads and tea sets. Steel was used for penknives and ice skates, sled runners and velocipedes. Wood was still popular for building blocks, stilts, sand funnels and log cabin construction sets. The population of New York was less than half a million in 1844, but there were already eighty-eight toy shops.

It was in the small toy shops of the Victorian era that a child could finally dream to his heart's content. The quality and variety of toys increased with the demand. There were such things as mechanical banks and wind-up toys, animated bell ringers and steam engines. But children still desired the simple toys that had amused their ancestors since the days of the pyramids, and shops were filled with traditional toys as well as new novelties.

For the miniature shop, you will need the shadow box, two shelf units, two display counters, a cash register, and a telephone from directions given before. The register counter is found in this chapter, and you will need a mirror, 5 inches long and 2¾ inches wide, for above this counter. You will also need a partition, 12 inches wide and 11 inches high, to separate the shop from the workshop. A doorway, 3 inches wide and 7 inches high with a curved top, should be cut into this partition 6 inches from the front edge. A gathered curtain should be made for this doorway. The partition should be secured 8 inches from the left side of the box. The toy shop should be wallpapered, while the workshop should be painted. Furnishings for the workshop are found in this chapter.

There are directions for most of the toys on the following pages, but toys, in miniature, take up very little room and we found additions to the toy shop in many unsuspecting places. Hoops were parts of earrings and a baby carriage was a candle holder. Craft shops had plastic miniatures and others were ordered from private dealers. You could spend years adding handmade items to this shop. Find a book on antique toys and think of ways to reproduce them.

Register Counter

In trying to give this shop a look that was different from the others, we separated the two shelf units with this counter for the cash register. Use ⅛-inch-thick basswood for this one (or balsa if you have been working with that for counters and shelves). Cut a countertop 2¾ inches wide by 2⅜ inches deep. Cut two side pieces, each 2 inches wide and 3 inches high. Cut a front piece 2¾ inches wide and 3 inches high. Glue the sides to the front piece (overlapping the front) and then beneath the countertop. To make sure the bottom keeps its shape, glue a piece 2½ inches wide by 2 inches deep and glue between the three sides about ½ inch from the bottom. Trim the front of the counter with ¼-inch-wide strips around the four edges and cut a center piece 1¾ inches wide and 2 inches high. Stain and varnish.

Workbench

Toymaking in America dates back to the seventeenth and eighteenth centuries when fathers whittled toys for their children in their rare spare moments. Some descendants of these Yankee craftsmen started toy shops in this country and continued the family pastime by making many of the toys they stocked. We have made this shopkeeper such a craftsman, and he can be seen putting the finishing touches on a sled at his workbench.

Use ⅛-inch-thick wood for the workbench. For the bench top, cut a piece 8¼ inches long and 2¾ inches wide. For the back, cut a piece 8 inches long and 4½ inches wide. For the base, cut a piece 7⅝ inches long and 2½ inches wide. The legs should be cut from ⅜-inch-square pieces and should each be 2¾ inches long. Cut 6 holes, ⅜ inch square, in the four corners and the center front and back of the bottom piece for the legs. Glue the base piece against the bottom of the back. Glue the top of the bench 2⅜ inches from the top of the back. To support these pieces, push the legs through the holes in the base piece and glue to the bottom of the bench top, leaving ½ inch beyond the base. To stabilize the top of the bench even further, cut a piece of wood 8 inches long and ⅜ inch wide. Glue beneath the bench top against the legs. Do the same on the sides with two piece of ⅜-inch-wide wood cut to a length of 2½ inches each. Glue into place on the sides. Do the same around the base of the bench, using a piece 8 inches long and ½ inch wide in the front and side pieces 2½ inches long and ½ inch wide. To hold the small tools (available from dealers) use a strip of leather 10 inches long and ¼ inch wide. Glue to the back of the bench, making small pockets for the tools to fit into.

An ice cream parlor, candy shop, and bakery are combined in this confectionery.

This Victorian confectionery front is typically fancy and reminds one of the frills that were popular during that era.

General stores with fronts like this were often located at major crossroads across the country.

The front of the one-room schoolhouse brings back memories with its pile of wood for the stove and the bell in the tower.

In the Victorian millinery, a fashionable woman considers a new hat.

Inside the general store, the owner tries to keep away summer flies as he waits for customers.

The one-room schoolhouse gives us a clear picture of education in an earlier day.

The toymaker is painting a sled to be sold in the toyshop.

This toy shop front shows us the toy shop on the right side and the recessed workshop on the left side.

The millinery looks soft and elegant in white and Williamsburg blue.

Register Counter

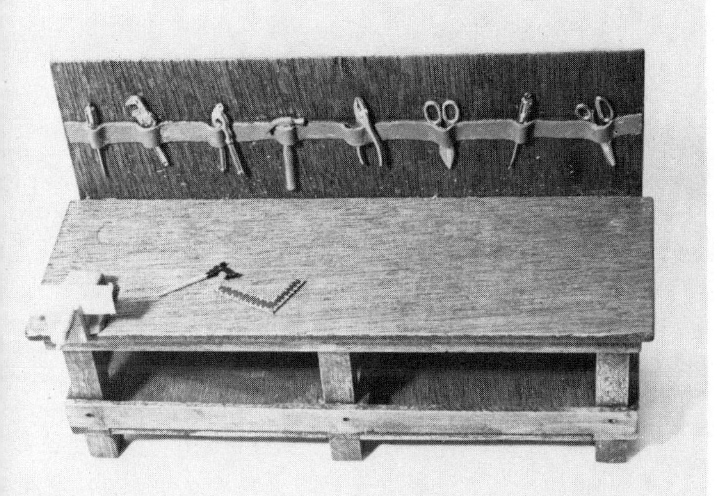

Workbench

Although toy factories were established during the Industrial Revolution in the early nineteenth century, many of the toy shop owners still made and repaired toys. Since our shopkeeper falls into this category, he needs a large supply of wood on hand for his projects and a place to store it.

For this wood supply box, use ⅛-inch-thick basswood. Cut two pieces, each 3½ inches long and 1¼ inches wide. Cut two more pieces, each 3½ inches long by ¾ inch wide. Cut two end pieces and a middle partition (3 pieces) each 1⅝ inches wide and 2½ inches high. Cut one base piece 3¼ inches long and 1⅝ inches wide. Glue the two end pieces to the ends of the base. Glue the thicker bottom front piece to the edges of all three pieces. Repeat in the back. Glue the top front piece into place and do the same on the back. Finally, glue the partition into place. Stain and varnish and fill with different-sized pieces of balsa wood.

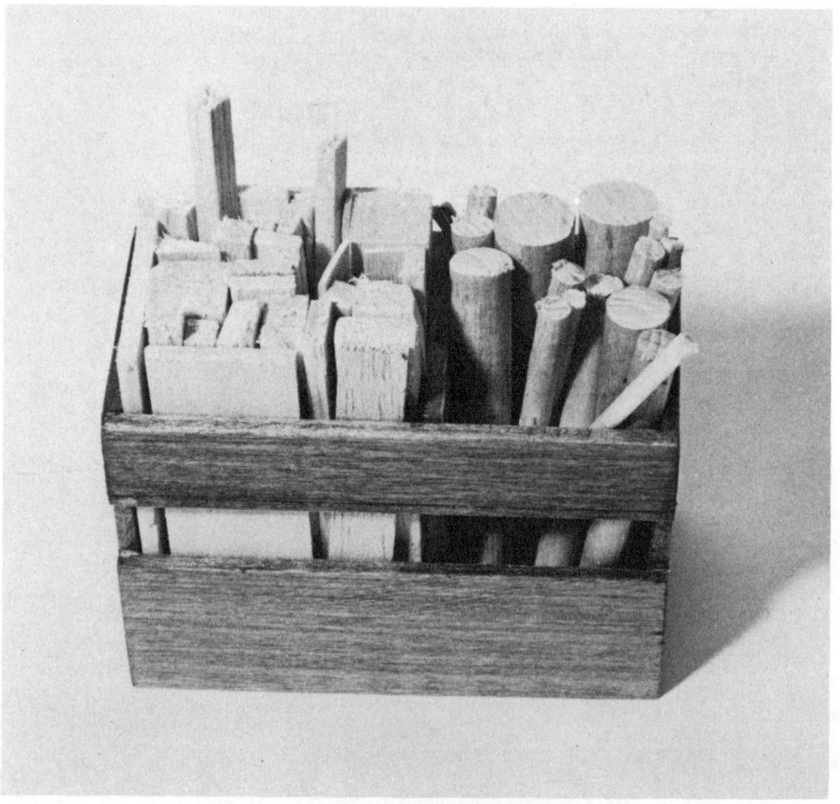

Wood Supply Box

Although turn-of-the century shop buildings did not have many windows, we decided to give the toymaker a small one for light and ventilation. Use balsa wood for the frame, using ¼-inch-wide strips for the outer frame and ⅛-inch-wide strips for the inner frame. For the outer frame, cut two pieces 3½ inches long for the top and bottom and two pieces 2½ inches long for the sides. Overlap the edges at a right angle, cut through the middle, and glue the four sides in a box shape onto a piece of clear acetate. For the inner window, cut four pieces 1¾ inches long and four pieces 1½ inches long from the ⅛-inch strips. Make two "windows" by gluing the 1½ inch pieces to the top and bottom strips on the inside of the window and the 1¾-inch pieces vertically between them. For the window handles, cut two small semicircles of balsa, paint gold, and glue into place as shown. When the frame is complete, find a picture that looks like a back alley and glue the window to the picture, trimming both the acetate and the picture when it is dry. Glue to the back wall of the workshop.

Toy Shop Window

One thing every toymaker needed was a large supply of paint since so many of the toys were made from wood. This shelf unit was devised to hold the cans.

Using ⅛-inch-thick wood, cut two pieces 1¾ inches long and 1 inch wide for the ends. Cut one back piece 1¾ inches high and 2¾ inches wide. Cut another back piece 1¾ inches high and 2¼ inches wide. Cut three pieces (for the top, middle, and bottom shelves on the right), each 2½ inches long and 1 inch wide. Cut three pieces for the left side, each 2 inches long and 1 inch wide. Cut the connecting edges of the two top shelves at a forty-five-degree angle. Do the same for the bottom pieces and the middle pieces. Glue the backs together at a right angle. Next glue the shelves together on the angle and glue them to the back, making the top shelf larger than the bottom one. Glue the ends in place. Cut paint cans from different sized dowels. Paint them gray and silver and add dots in various colors to show the color of the paint. Glue to the shelves.

Shelf with Paint Cans

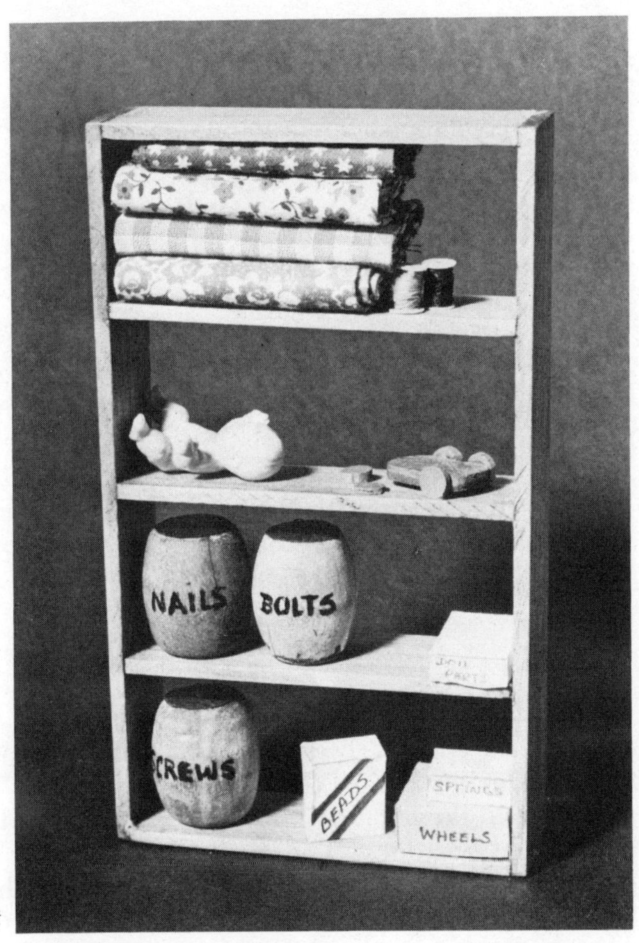

Storage Unit

Storage Unit

Storage is always a problem in a workshop area, and a toymaker can never have too much space. For this storage unit, use ⅛-inch-thick basswood. Cut two side pieces, each 6 inches long 1 inch wide. Cut five shelves, each 3¼ inches long and 1 inch wide. Space the shelves an equal distance apart and glue between the sides. Stain and varnish the unit. Using the directions for bolts of cloth and spools of thread found in the general store chapter, make some to fit the top shelf. Put a small doll and a half-finished wagon on another. Use wooden beads for kegs and cover the tops with circles of black construction paper. Make various-sized boxes (basic directions in the millinery chapter) for the other loose parts every toymaker would need.

Backgammon and Parcheesi

A playing board suitable for playing backgammon was found at Ur and may date back to 3000 B.C. The ancient Greeks and Romans played a "twelve-lined game" nearly identical to backgammon. In 1743, Edmond Hoyle codified the rules in a book published in England. By comparison, parcheesi is a relatively new game even though it has been manufactured for more than one hundred years. It was first marketed in 1867.

For a backgammon board, cut a piece of white matting board 1¾ inches square. Frame as shown with ⅛-inch square balsa that has been stained a wood color. With black and red felt-tipped pens, draw the twelve lines as shown, alternating red and black.

For the parcheesi board, use white matting board again and cut a 1½ inch square. Draw the board as shown (or use a contemporary one as a guide). Color with felt-tipped pens.

Dart Board and Checkers

We have reports of darts being thrown at a tournament practice target as far back as the sixteenth century. They were also a pastime for the Pilgrims aboard the *Mayflower* in 1620. The game of checkers goes much farther back and may be one of the world's oldest intellectual pastimes. There are records of the game of checkers being played in the days of the earlier Pharaohs. Plato and Homer both mention the game in their works, and it is thought that the Romans imported the game from Greece. The first book of rules for the game was published in Spain in 1547.

For the dart board, use a quarter for a pattern, and cut out a circle from a ⅛-inch-thick piece of balsa. Make another circle the same size on plain white paper. Draw a dart board pattern and color with felt tipped pens. Cut out the circle and glue onto the circle of wood. Paint the edge of the wood black. For darts, use the ends of small nails. Roll thin, colored tissue paper around the edge, leaving enough to make slits in for the feather effect. Push into the dart board.

For the checker board, cut a piece of white matting board 1 inch square. With a black felt-tipped pen, divide the board into sixty-four squares (eight on each line). Color alternating ones red and black. For the box of checkers, use a piece of wood ⅝ inch long by ⅜ inch high and ¼ inch wide. Paint black. Glue a piece of white paper to the top with the word *checkers* written on it.

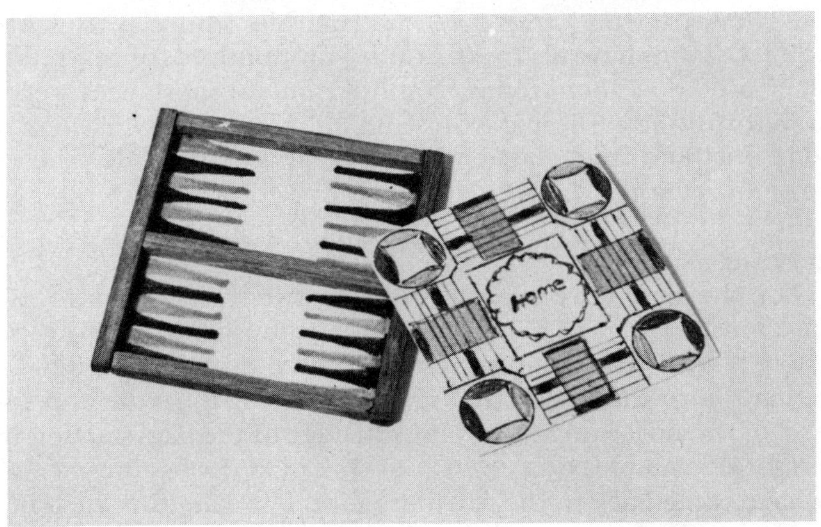

Backgammon and Parcheesi

Dart Board and Checkers

Marbles and Crayons

Marbles were found in an Egyptian child's grave dating back to the fourth millennium B.C. They used to be made of jasper or agate. Round pellets of clay were also found in England dating from 312 B.C. and Roman children played with marbles around 27 B.C. In the

United States, the *Boy's Own Book* rated marbles from clay to alabaster in 1829. Crayons have also been around for hundreds of years but not quite as we know them today. Natural mineral substances were cut into sticks for the earliest crayons, and most of the early masters such as da Vinci and Michelangelo used natural crayons. By the early nineteenth century, fabricated materials with a waxy binder were substituted for the natural crayons, and contemporary crayons came into being.

For the miniature marble bag, cut two ¾-inch-square pieces from a finished edge of material. Using the finished edge for the top, make a ⅛-inch seam along the other three edges with right sides together. Turn the bag to the right side. Using a needle and single strand of thread, seam around the top edge of the bag, starting from the right side and leaving an inch of thread at the beginning. When you have come back to the starting point, leave another inch of the thread, cut off the rest and tie the two ends together. Do the same from the left side so that you have a draw string on either side. Make tiny marbles of Repla-Cotta, bake, paint, and place in the bag. Pull the draw strings and you are ready to display the bag of marbles.

For the crayon box, start with 1/16-inch-thick balsa and cut a base ⅝ inch long by ⅜ inch wide. From 1/16-inch-thick and ⅛-inch-wide balsa strips, cut four sides and glue into the shape of a box. Paint yellow and use black for the word *crayon* on the front. For the crayons themselves, use round toothpicks. Paint the ends of three toothpicks six different colors. While they are drying, make thin lines with fine-tipped felt pens on a sheet of white paper for 5/16 inch. When the toothpicks are dry, glue small pieces of this colored paper around the end of the toothpick, making sure that a colored tip is left showing. Cut each crayon to a length of ⅜ inch and glue into the box.

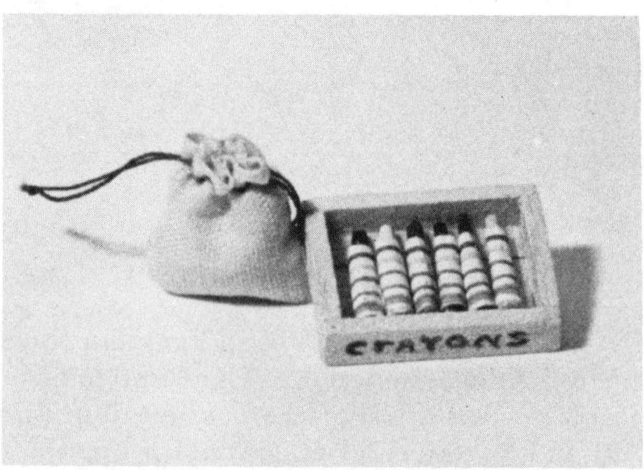

Marbles and Crayons

Jack-in-the-boxes were known in the sixteenth century and were mentioned by Rousseau in his writings. Mr. Punch, an early favorite, reached the United States about 1825, and by the Victorian era there were many variations.

For these jack-in-the-boxes, start with ½-inch-square balsa wood. Cut pieces for the bases ½ inch long each. For the open lids, use 1/16-inch-thick balsa and cut pieces ½ inch square. Glue to the top of the base and paint the base and the lid red. For the flounces at the clown's neck use ¼-inch-wide green ribbon. Cut a 1¾-inch long piece for each flounce. Sew the ends together. Then gather the

Jack-in-the-Boxes

inner edge and pull together tightly to form a circle. The jack-in-the-boxes may be made one of two ways. As shown in the one on the left, you may use a small, round, wooden bead and a small nail. Glue the bead to the top of the nail. Paint the facial features and hair on the bead. Then pass the nail through the neck flounce into the top of the base. Decorate the base with squares and letters of the alphabet with white and green paint. The winding handle is a nail pounded into an S shape. Clip off the head of the nail and push into the right side of the box.

To make the jack-in-the-box on the right, start with the same basic box and neck flounce, but instead of using a nail, cut a 2-inch piece of thin wire. Fold around a toothpick, leaving a straight piece ¼ inch long at each end. Push one end into the middle of the base. Put the flounce over the other end, but do not push down over the circles of wire. Top with a larger bead glued onto the wire. Make a pointed hat for the clown from a piece of green felt. Glue into place and paint the features of the clown and the design around the base. Add the winding handle as before.

Animal Pulltoys

In ancient Persia, 1100 years before Christ, limestone toy animals with holes for pulling them were placed in a temple cornerstone to be unearthed hundreds of years later. Other animal pulltoys survive from ancient Egypt and Greece. Pulltoys fascinated children for hundreds of years and were still a big favorite during the Victorian era.

For the yellow bird, use ⅛-inch-thick balsa wood. Cut a base piece ¾ inch long by ½ inch wide. Round off the edges. With sandpaper, carve the bird form out of a piece of ⅛ inch balsa cut to a length of ⅝ inch and a height of ½ inch. Gauge a small hole for the bird in the base ⅝ inch long. Paint the base blue and the bird yellow. Use black paint for the bird's eye and wing. When dry, glue the bird into the hole in the base. For wheels, cut small circles from a ¼-inch-in-diameter

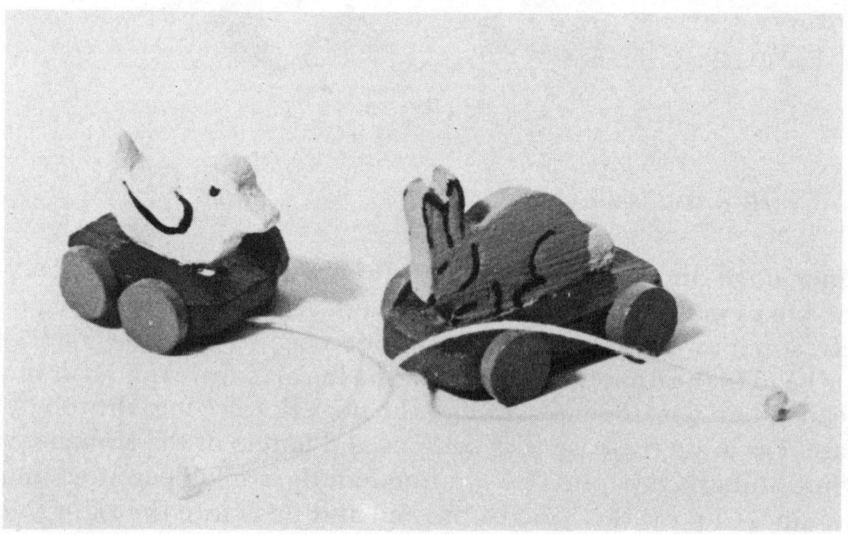

Animal Pulltoys

dowel. Paint them red and glue into place. For the string, cut a piece of thread 1¾ inches long. Tie one end to a small bead. Make a small hole in the front of the base of the toy and glue the other end of the thread into place.

For the rabbit, use ⅛-inch-thick balsa again and cut a base piece 1 inch long and ½ inch wide. The rabbit should be cut from a piece ¾ inch long by ½ inch high. Carve with sandpaper again. Gauge the base as before with a ¾ inch hole for the rabbit. Paint the base green, the rabbit brown, the tail white, and use black to outline the rabbit. Glue the rabbit into place and make four wheels from the ¼ inch dowel and paint red before gluing into place. Cut another piece of thread 1¾ inches long and make the pull string as before.

Kites

Kites were used for military signaling in China as early as 206 B.C. By medieval times, they were established as children's toys as seen in the woodcuts of the period. Kite flying later became a national sport in the East with bets being laid on prospective winners.

For the miniature kite, use thin, colored tissue paper. Cut a 2½-inch piece of 1/16-inch-square balsa stripping and glue to the

Kite

tissue. Cut two more pieces, each ¾ inch long, and glue to either side of the middle piece ¾ inch from the top. Cut two more pieces each 1¼ inch long, and glue between the top and sides of the kite to form the top part. Cut two more pieces, each 2 inches long, and glue between the bottom tip and the sides. Leaving an edge of 3/16 inch, cut around the kite. Fold the 3/16-inch tissue paper onto the back rim of the kite and glue into place. For the tail, use a strip of white ribbon 4½ inches long. Glue to the back of the kite. Tie four smaller strips along this tail. For the string holder, use a ⅜-inch-long piece of rounded balsa. Stain. Glue and wrap thread around this holder and when you have enough, pass the loose end through the middle of the kite with a needle and glue to the back. Make several kites in different colors to hang on the wall of the shop.

Paint Box and Books

The art of painting has fascinated man since his creation. Along with fossils of early man dating from the Paleolithic period are the cave paintings that remain as proof of his creativity. This creative expression has been passed down through the generations, and a paint set has been a welcomed gift for hundreds of years. Interesting children's books are a much newer phenomenon. In 1691, we had John Cotton's *Spiritual Milk for Boston Babes*, but it was not until *Mother Goose* was published in Boston in 1719, followed closely by *Robinson Crusoe* and *Gulliver's Travels,* that Americans got something to stir the child's imagination. By 1762, *Warner's Almanac* offered a great variety of Play-Books for children.

For a miniature paint box, use ⅛-inch-thick wood. Cut a base ¾ inch long and ⅜ inch wide. Using ¼-inch-wide strips, cut two pieces ¾ inch long and two pieces ⅝ inch long. Glue to the base to form a box shape, overlapping the sides. Cut another piece of the ¼-inch-wide strip to a length of ¾ inch and glue flat inside the box for the paint platform. Cut a box lid 1 inch long by ⅝ inch wide. Cut a piece of white paper 1 inch square. Glue to the top of the lid and the back of the box for a hinge. Paint the whole box including the paper silver. Paint different-colored circles on the platform for the paints. Make a small brush from a round toothpick, painting it red with a black tip. Place in the pocket behind the platform. This item is larger than the 1-inch scale but still looks cute on the shelves.

For miniature books, look in catalogs and magazines for pictures of children's books. Glue to cardboard and stand on the shelves or spread out on the countertops.

Paint Box and Books

Blocks, Top, and Windmill

Building blocks were first described in London in 1653, and by 1844 they were being made with pictures on them. By the second half of the nineteenth century, alphabet picture making blocks were being printed by chromo-litho in the United States. Tops have endured as one of our oldest toys. The Greeks had them in 579 B.C., while the Romans played with them as early as 27 B.C. During the sixteenth century, grownups developed a liking for them, and by the Victorian era there were many variations. There were whipping tops and humming tops, catching tops and fighting tops. The top was clearly here to stay. Windmills do not date back quite as far, although they were popular in medieval times and appear in manuscripts and early woodcuts. During the 1800s, they were popular toys at fairs in England where you could buy a paper windmill for a penny.

For miniature blocks, use balsa strips that are ⅜ inch square. Paint two opposite sides of the strips white. Paint the other two sides red and green. When dry, cut into tiny blocks (⅜ inch square) and paint the remaining two sides blue and yellow. Paint letters of the alphabet on some blocks and glue tiny pictures of toys on others. Glue together as shown or make your own arrangement.

For the top, start with a wooden bead about ⅝ inch in diameter.

Try to find one with one end slightly more pointed than the other. Push the top of a toothpick through the hole in the bead and glue into place, breaking off the top about ⅛ inch above the hole. Paint the bead and toothpick red. Wind and glue thread to the top part of the toothpick to look like the string you would pull.

For the paper windmill, start with a piece of construction paper ½ inch square. Make four slits from the corners toward the middle of the paper and fold the alternating tips toward the middle. For the stick, use 1/16-inch-square balsa and cut a piece 1½ inches long. Paint blue. Push a tiny nail through the middle (catching four corners) of the windmill and into the top of the stick. Snip off the edge of the nail. For special effects, you may want to paint the edges of the paper windmill blue or any color to match your stick handle.

Blocks, Top, and Windmill

Sled

Although sleds antedate the Christian era, they were still popular as the first settlers came to America. By the late 1800s, ten to fifteen thousand were made and painted yearly at the Crandall toy factory on Third Avenue in New York. The first steering sled, the American Flexible Flyer, appeared in 1889.

For the miniature sled, use ⅛-inch-thick basswood or balsa wood cut to ¼-inch widths. Cut three pieces, each 2¼ inches long. Cut two more pieces, each 1¼ inches long. Line up the three long pieces side by side. Starting ¾ inch from each end, glue the two shorter pieces

Sled

across the long pieces. Using ¼-inch-square wood, cut two more pieces 1¼ inch long. Glue these beside the other shorter pieces ¼ inch from each end of the long pieces. For the rungs, use ⅛-inch-thick wood again. Cut and shape rungs from pieces 3 inches long by ½ inch wide. Glue to the edges of the ¼-inch square pieces. Paint the whole sled red.

Bat, Baseball, and Football

The official game of baseball got its start in 1839 when Abner Doubleday laid out the game for his pupils at a military school in Cooperstown, New York. By the late nineteenth century, it had grown to national stature, and most young boys wanted a bat and ball to imitate their professional hero. Although balls antedate the Christian era, footballs have some interesting history behind them. In Shakespeare's time, footballs were made of leather with a sheep's bladder inside. In America, boys were not allowed to play football in the streets of Boston in 1657 since it was considered a "bloody" game.

For a miniature baseball bat, use a ⅜-inch-square balsa strip and cut a piece 2½ inches long. With sandpaper, carve the shape of a baseball bat like the one shown in the picture. Varnish for a smooth finish. Make a baseball ¼ inch in diameter from Repla-Cotta. Bake, paint white, and then add black lines for the stitching.

The football shown was sanded into shape from a piece of balsa wood ½ inch thick and 1 inch long. It was then painted brown and, when dry, the white stitching was added with white paint. This football may also be made from the Repla-Cotta, baked, and then painted.

Bat, Ball, and Football

Noah's Ark and Sailboat

A Noah's Ark was known as the "Sunday toy." In Colonial America the Sabbath was observed and toys were put away, except the Ark, which had religious significance. Arks can be traced back to the late sixteenth century in Germany, although some of the best made in America were made by the Pennsylvania Dutch in the eighteenth to nineteenth centuries. Toy sailboats were especially popular during the later part of the nineteenth century. Around 1899 it was the thing to do to take a summer vacation at the seashore. Sailor suits were popular and most boys possessed a sailboat to take along to float in the waves.

For the Noah's Ark, start with a ½-inch-thick balsa strip. Cut a piece 1¼ inches long and ¾ inch wide. With sandpaper, carve the shape of the bottom of the ark, tapering it to a point in the front. For the house on top of the boat, cut a piece of balsa ⅜ inch wide, ¾ inch long, and $^{5}/_{16}$ inch high. Taper the two sides of the top to hold the roof cut from ⅛-inch-thick balsa. Cut two pieces, each ¾ inch long by ¼ inch wide. Bevel the top edges and glue on top of the house. Glue the house on top of the boat and decorate.

For the sailboat, use 1/16-inch-thick wood. Cut a base 1 inch long and ⅜ inch wide. Taper the front into a boat shape. Cut a 1-inch length of 1/16-inch-square strip of balsa. Make a small hole in the front of the boat and glue into place to hold the sail. For the sail, use white construction paper. Cut a piece ⅞ inch high and ⅝ inch wide at the bottom. Glue onto the balsa strip and paint a number at the top. Paint the boat base blue and make several for the shelves in different colors.

Noah's Ark and Sailboat

Dollhouse with Front

The first dollhouses were luxury toys for the wealthy. The earliest one on record was ordered by Duke Albrecht V of Bavaria for his daughter in 1558. It was four stories high with seventeen doors, sixty-three windows, a stable, and a ballroom. There were silver and gold dishes, rich tapestries, spinning wheels, silver lutes, and many other fine accessories, which finally convinced the duke to put it into his art collection instead. By the Victorian era, there were dollhouses being made for children in factories as well as by well-intentioned fathers. Large toy stores such as Schwarz sold elaborate accessories, and many Victorian little girls learned the basics of housekeeping from this useful toy.

For the closed dollhouse, use ⅛-inch-thick wood. Cut a base piece 2 inches long and 1¼ inches wide. Cut two pieces for the front and back of the dollhouse 1¾ inches wide and 1 inch high. Cut two end pieces 1½ inch high by ¾ inch wide. On these end pieces, measure 1 inch along the long side and from that point on both sides, make slits that meet in the middle of the shorter edge, forming a V shape for the roof. Glue the front and back to the sides (overlapping the front and back) and glue onto the base. Bevel the edges of the front and back to match the roof line. Cut two more pieces of the ⅛-inch-thick wood for the roof, cutting one 2⅛ inches long and 1 inch wide and the other 2⅛ inches long and ⅞ inch wide. Glue the large one on first, leaving ⅛ inch overlap at the top onto which you should glue the other side of the roof. For the pillars, use ⅛ inch in diameter dowels, cutting to fit under the roof. Paint the dollhouse white, the roof red, the grass green, the windows and doors black, and the shutters blue. Green shrubbery may be added.

Dollhouse with Front

Hobbyhorse and Tumbling Clown

The hobbyhorse is one of the world's oldest toys. The children of Socrates were supposed to have had a hobbyhorse as did the Chinese children during the Ming Dynasty. It was such a favorite during the Middle Ages that a fifteenth century manuscript even shows the child Jesus playing on one. Tumbling toys were derived from the Far East where tilting figures were originally made to represent meditators. As the toy developed, the figures became friendlier, some even comical.

For the hobbyhorse, start with a ⅛-inch-in-diameter dowel. Cut a piece 2½ inches long. For the head, use ½-inch-square balsa wood. Cut a piece 1 inch long and sand into shape as shown. Drill a small hole in the base of the neck for the stick and glue the stick into place. Use 1/16-inch-square strips of balsa for the handles, cutting 2 pieces, each ¼ inch long. Make a small hole on either side of the horse's head, and glue the handles into place. Paint the handles and the stick blue, the horse's head white. The mane should be brown, while red should be used for the bridle and black for the horse's features.

The tumbling clown is made from two beads. The body is a red bead (or a wooden one painted red) ⅝ inch in diameter, while the head is a white bead 5/16 inch in diameter. Glue the white bead on top of the red one and glue a piece of gold cord around the neck. The pointed hat was made from a piece of red suede, rolled into the shape of a hat and glued into place. Gold paint was used to outline the mittens and buttons, while blue paint was used for the mittens. Black paint was used for the facial features.

Hobbyhorse and Tumbling Clown

Jump Rope and Stilts

Jump ropes were popular in the Victorian era when children were supposed to be seen and not heard. Anything that took the child outdoors, such as a swing or a ball, was in vogue. Stilts were another favorite, although they were originally designed for crossing rivers and marshes. The city of Namur in Belgium was famous for its stilt walkers, since it was often flooded by two nearby rivers.

For a jump rope, cut a 6-inch length of gold cord. Glue the ends into two long, thin, red beads and hang on the wall of the toy shop.

For stilts, use ⅛-inch-square balsa strips. Cut two pieces, each 5 inches long. Make ledges for the feet from ⅛-inch-thick balsa. Cut two pieces, each ⅜ inch wide by ½ inch long. Shape as shown and glue to one side of the poles, ¾ inch from the bottom. Varnish.

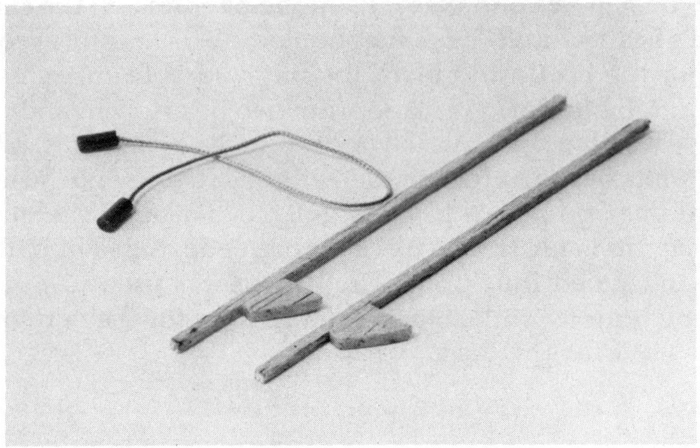

Jump Rope and Stilts

Drum and Paddleball

Drums had their origin in ritual magic, although they have served many purposes through the centuries. They have provided court music as well as the rhythm for dancing and marching. They were represented in medieval European paintings, and by the thirteenth century three types of drums were already developed. Many toys remind us of adult games, and this paddleball is certainly one of them. Tennis or the adult game of paddleball are quickly brought to mind.

For the drum, use a ¾-inch-thick dowel cut to a length of ⅝ inch. Paint the two ends white and the middle green with red strings. For the drumsticks, use two flat toothpicks cut to a length of 1 inch each. Paint gold and glue to the top. Make several.

The paddleball is made from ⅛-inch-thick balsa. Form the paddle with sandpaper from a piece 1 inch long and ½ inch wide. Varnish. When dry, knot one end of a piece of white thread and, with a needle, pass it through the middle of the racket until it is 1¾ inches long. Tie a small bead to the end and place on a counter.

Drum and Paddleball

Rocking Horse

Rocking horses were made for the children of the wealthy in England in the early 1600s. By 1785, an English cabinet maker named William Long had arrived in the United States and had put an ad in the *Pennsylvania Packet* saying that he made rocking horses in the "neatest and best manner."

For this rocking horse, start with a ½-inch dowel. Cut a piece 1¼ inches long. Using a ⅛-inch dowel, cut four legs, each 1⅛ inches long. Drill four small holes in the bottom of the dowel and glue the legs into place. Carve the head out of a ⅛-inch-thick piece of wood 1½ inches high and 1¼ inches wide. The tail piece is ¾ inch high and ½ inch wide. Make notches in the top front and rear of the horse's dowel body and glue the head and tail into place. For the rocker base, cut the rockers and base out of ⅛-inch-thick wood. Make the platform 1⅜ inches long by 1¼ inches wide. Cut two rockers out of the same thickness wood cut to a length of 2 inches and a width of 1 inch. Make

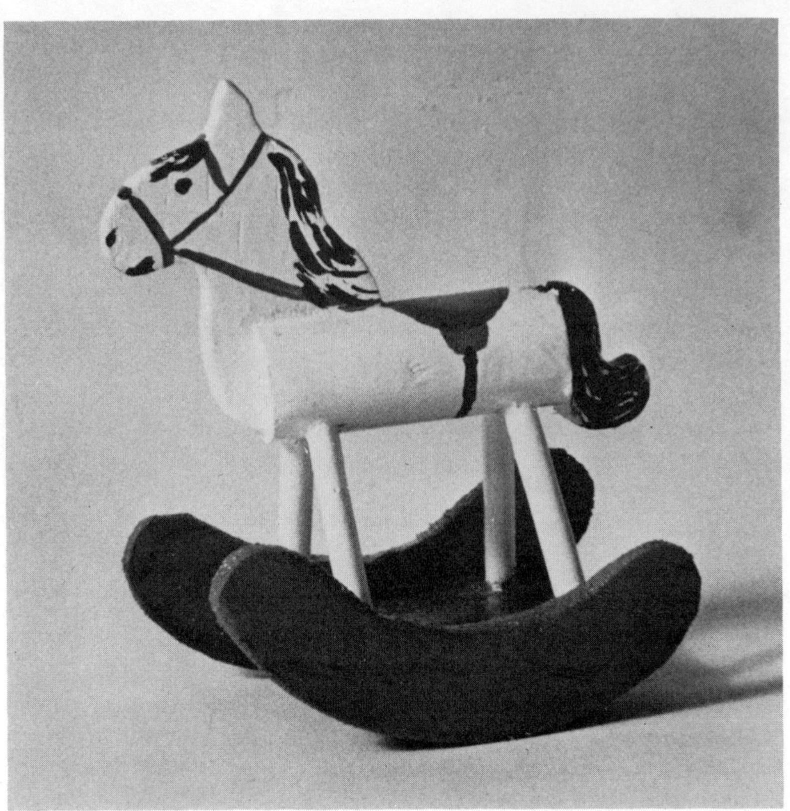

Rocking Horse

four holes in the base piece and glue the horse's legs into place. Finally, glue the base between the rockers, making sure the horse is centered so that it will rock. Paint the base and rockers red and the horse white. The features, mane, and tail of the horse should be black, while the saddle and bridle should be red.

Wagon

In ancient Mesopotamia, four-wheeled wagons were used in the third millennium B.C. During the same period, they were also used as covered wagons for family travel by the Asian nomads. The wagon reached Europe during the late Bronze Age, and through the ages they have been used for everything from hearses to toys.

This toy wagon is made from ⅛-inch-thick wood. Cut two side pieces, each 1⅞ inches long and ⅝ inch wide. Cut two end pieces, each ⅞ inch long by ⅝ inch wide. Cut a base ⅞ inch wide and 1⅝ inches long. Glue the four sides around the base, forming a box by overlapping the long sides on the ends. Using 3/16-inch-wide strips, cut the trim for the top of the wagon. Cut two pieces each 2 inches long, and 2 pieces each 1⅛ inches long. Glue to the upper rim of the wagon. Cut two more pieces of this 3/16-inch-wide strip into two pieces, each 1⅛ inches long, and glue beneath the wagon for the wheels. Carve four wheels, each ⅜ inch in diameter (or cut from dowels), and nail to the strips beneath the wagon. For the handle, cut one more piece of the 3/16-inch-wide wood to a length of 1¾ inches. Cut the heads off two small nails and hammer into the end for a handle. Sand the other end of this piece at an angle and glue onto the wagon as shown. Paint the wagon red, the wheels black, and the handle silver.

Wagon

Open Dollhouse and Doll

Although the seventeenth-century "baby houses" were really display cabinets for the miniatures of the adults, the clusters of rooms gave future generations a pattern for dollhouses. During the latter part of the eighteenth century, the baby house evolved from a piece of furniture to a toy as the exteriors were made to look more realistic. By the end of the nineteenth century, dollhouses were mass produced, and many types of homes were imitated from the cottage to the townhouse.

The first dolls were not toys but idols to be worshipped or images of sorcerers in witchcraft. Some were used as burial figures, others as fertility symbols. As civilizations advanced, children got dolls, and ancient Egypt left us samples in ivory, wax, and even fabric. Dolls enjoyed a popularity in ancient Greece and Rome that was not revived until the nineteenth century. Through the Middle Ages, we find a few formal figures of wax or wood, often sold by traveling peddlers. By the eighteenth century, doll making was again a major industry, and the Industrial Revolution brought dolls of papier-mâché, wax, and even china. In the nineteenth century, dolls were given realistic features, and the Victorian child had a wide range of choices from babies to fashion dolls.

For this open dollhouse, use 1/16-inch-thick wood. Cut three pieces for the bottom and middle floors and the upper ceiling 3/8 inch wide and 1½ inches long. Cut two side pieces 3/8 inch wide and 2 inches long. Cut two room dividers 3/8 inch wide and 11/16 inch long. For the roof, cut two pieces ¼ inch wide and 1¾ inches long. Finally, cut a back piece 1⅝ inches square. Make a V-shaped cut 3/8 inch long on one end of each of the side pieces for the peaked roof. Glue the two floor and the ceiling pieces between the sides with the divider walls centered between them. Glue this frame onto the back of the dollhouse. Sand the top edge of the back so that the roof will fit smoothly over the sides and back. Bevel one of the edges of each of the roof pieces and glue together over the sides. Paint the house

Open Dollhouse and Doll

white, the roof red, and add pieces of construction paper for the carpeting.

For the doll, use a small, wooden bead for the head. Fill the hole with a filler like Wood Dough and paint on the hair and features. For the body, use a flexible wire cut to a length of about 7 inches. Shape the body with the single strand of wire, starting in the hole of the bead for the neck, making one arm, the body, legs, the other arm, and finally ending up back at the neck, which should be glued into the bead. For hands and feet, use Repla-Cotta. Cover the ends of the hands and feet and bake for ten minutes until hard. When cool, paint a wood color. Make a small dress for the doll and seat on the shelf.

Teddy Bear and Ball

In 1802, while in Mississippi to settle a boundary dispute, Teddy Roosevelt went bear hunting. He set his aim for a cub but refused to shoot it. The story became popular, and Morris Michton, a Russian immigrant and toymaker in Brooklyn, created a stuffed bear and called it Teddy's Bear. This was the first of many to come.

The ball is the earliest known toy. Stone balls were carved around 2000 B.C., and plaited rush balls are pictured on wall paintings in Egypt from 1786 B.C. Homer mentioned balls in the Odyssey in 860 B.C., and much later in history, seven-year-old Edward V played handball as a prisoner in the tower of London.

This miniature teddy bear is made from imitation fur. Cut out the pieces, using the following pattern:

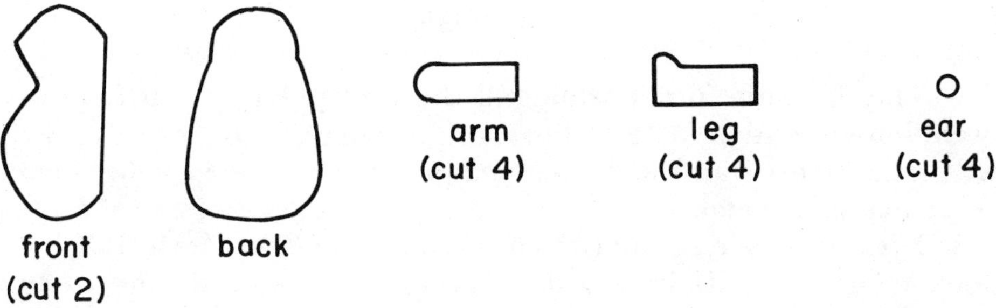

Sew the front of the two front pieces together, stuff, and sew the sides that are left to the back piece. Sew the arms and legs together (remembering to stuff) and sew to the body. Finally, sew the ears together and sew into place. Use tiny circles of yellow felt with black pen dots for the eyes, and stitch a small yellow nose on the pointed tip of the face. For a final touch, tie a narrow strand of red suedecloth around the bear's neck.

For the ball, use Repla-Cotta and shape into a large ball. Bake as directed. When cool, paint with red acrylic paint.

Teddy Bear and Ball

Wooden Train

The Stockton and Darlington, the first public steam railway, went into operation in 1825, but there weren't any toy trains before 1840. Large toy trains were then made of wood, while smaller ones were made of metal.

For this wooden train (which is larger than the 1-inch scale but looks cute on a shelf), use wood that is ⅝ inch thick for the three rear cars. Cut three pieces, each 1 inch long and ⅝ inch high. Using ⅛-inch-thick wood for the bases, cut four pieces, each 1¼ inch long and ⅝ inch wide. Glue the tops of the cars to the middle of the platforms (saving one for the engine). Curve the tops of the cars with sandpaper and round the edges of the platforms as well. Drill small holes into both ends of the platforms. For wheels, use a ⅜-inch dowel and cut sixteen wheels ⅛ inch thick. Attach to the cars with small nails, leaving enough room for them to turn. For the engine, use the remaining platform. From ¼-inch-thick wood, cut another base 1 inch long and ⅝ inch wide. Glue to the platform, matching one side for the front. Cut another piece of this same thickness wood ⅝ inch square. Glue in an upright position onto the back of the first piece. In front of this, glue half of a ½-inch-thick dowel. Round off the top of the engineer's compartment and the front of the train. Drill two small holes for the light and chimney and fill with short pieces of dowels. Add the wheels as you did for the cars. Paint the engine red and each of the cars a different color. Add windows with black paint and paint the wheels and chimney and light black. Use staples to attach the cars to one another.

Wooden Train

Wheelbarrow

The invention of the wheel gave rise to many things. There were chariots and carts and finally wheelbarrows to make transporting items easier from one place to another. Toy wheelbarrows were popular with children who liked to imitate adults.

For the wheelbarrow, start with ⅛-inch-thick wood. Cut a bottom piece 1¾ inches wide, 1½ inches long, and tapered to 1¼ inches at the other end. Cut two side pieces 1½ inches long and ½ inch high. Cut a back piece 1½ inches long and ½ inch high and a front piece 1 inch wide and ½ inch high. Glue the sides to the bottom of the wheelbarrow. Next glue the front between the sides, leaving a ⅛ inch margin along the front. Glue the back in place leaving the same margin. For the handles, use wood ¼ inch wide and cut two pieces, each 3½ inches long. Cut two legs, each ¾ inch long. Cut a wheel ¾ inch in diameter. Carve one end of each of the handles as shown. Drive a nail through the opposite end of the handle, then through the middle of the wheel, and finally through the other handle end. Glue the handles beneath the wheelbarrow as shown and glue the legs under the wheelbarrow on the inside of the handle pieces. Paint the wheel black, the handles and legs red, and the wheelbarrow green.

Wheelbarrow

4

1915 Confectionery Shop

Confectioneries, which were a combination ice cream parlor, candy shop, and bakery, were common in cities around the turn of the century. At the Smithsonian Institution, you'll find a room-sized display of the Stohlman's Confectionery Shop from 1911. A housewife could go there to buy her baked goods or candy treats for the children, while the whole family could visit the parlor area for a treat. Young men would splurge on banana splits for themselves and their girlfriends after a movie, while children favored the sundaes or floats made with syrup and carbonated water. The ice cream cone had been introduced at the 1904 World's Fair in St. Louis and was becoming a popular treat to take home along with the lollipops and candy sticks. There were gift boxes of candy for the man who was courting and individual pastries for special occasions. The confectionery would endure for many decades. There would be a great rise in business during Prohibition when substitutes were sought for alcoholic entertainment. The Depression would hurt confectioneries as it hurt everything else, but man's ageless desire for sweets would assure the shops a permanent place in our heritage.

For a miniature confectionery, you will need the basic shadow box, long counter, short counter, showcase, one shelf unit, and a door. Among the smaller items, you will need the clock, cash register, paper roll, string holder, and scales. The shop should be painted white. The parlor area should be papered part way down with a chair rail of thin balsa wood stained fruitwood running around the area. A chair rail may also be added to the right side of the shop. To make the setting more interesting, we made the eating area one step higher

Confectionery

than the store, as they did in the Stohlman Confectionery. We also added a room divider, and directions for both of these are in the following chapter.

When you have made the counters and shelves as shown in chapter 1, arrange the shelf and long counter on the back wall with the showcase in front of the shelf and the short counter in front of the long one as shown. Arrange the cash register and other accessories and you have the basic confectionery, which you will be able to fill with the items made from directions on the following pages.

Repla-Cotta was used for all the items in the baked goods section because it is soft and easy to mold, but hardens without shrinking when it is baked for ten minutes in a 300-degree oven. If you are used to working with bread dough or Play-Doh, you may also use these products. The candy jar directions are found in the general store chapter. The baked goods were displayed on buttons with doilies cut from full-sized ones and trays were cut from heavy-weight aluminum foil.

Platform

At the Stohlman Confectionery in the Smithsonian, we found a raised platform floor in the eating area that seemed to make it more interesting, and we adopted the idea for the miniature confectionery.

For the platform, you will need a piece of ¾-inch hardwood cut to 8⅞ inches by 11⅞ inches. To make smooth edges on the front and side, use ⅛-inch-thick basswood. For the front (which is really the right side on the picture), cut a piece ¾ inch wide and 9 inches long. Glue to the front of the platform. For the right side (in the top of the photo so you can see doorway cuts), cut a piece 1 inch wide by 12 inches long. On one side of this strip of wood, make ¼ inch deep cuts for the doorways in the divider. Starting 1¼ inches from one end, make a cut 2⅛ inches long and ¼ inch deep. Measure off 3⅝ inches after this and then make another cut the same size. When finished, glue to the right side of the platform. Paint the top and two edges dark brown and glue the oak trim flooring into place as you did before.

Platform

Divider

A room divider gives privacy and they were often used in sweet shops to separate the eating area from the more commercial bakery section.

For this divider, use masonite caning (also referred to as corrugated hardboard) in the pattern shown. Although it is usually sold in large sheets at lumber stores, you may be able to find a small piece in their leftover pile. For the shop you should cut a piece 12 inches long by 10¼ inches high, using the picture as a guide since a border should be left on the front and top. Cut two spaces for doors,

Divider

each 5½ inches high by 2⅛ inches wide, using the straight lines for the frames. If you are using a different pattern, you should put your first door 1¼ inch from the left edge, leaving 3⅝ inches in the middle, and then another door.

To secure the divider in the shop, glue to the top right edge of the ledge on the bottom. On the back wall, the divider should be held in place between two ¼-inch strips that have been stained and varnished.

Ice Cream Parlor Table

Turn-of-the-century confectioneries had one of two major types of tables. They had either the marble-topped wooden tables or the tables with the wrought-iron legs, which was the type chosen to be reproduced in our miniature shop.

Basswood was used for the table tops and chair seats, but balsa wood may also be used. With our basswood, we used a power saw and an attachment that made circles in wood. (With balsa, you would cut the wood with an X-acto knife and sand into a perfect circle.) The table tops are 1¾ inches in diameter. If you use such an attachment, you will have a hole in the middle of the piece. Fill with plastic wood dough. Let dry and sand smooth. To hold the legs, you will need a piece of balsa wood 1 inch square and at least ⅛ inch thick. Glue to the middle of the bottom of the table top. For the legs, use plumbers wire. You will need 5½ inches to make each 2-inch leg, although I recommend that you start with a longer piece and cut off the excess. Fold the wire in half, leaving a small circle for the foot of the leg. Since the wire is hard to bend, let someone hold the circle with a pair of pliers. Fold the wire from left to right until you have a 2¼-inch piece, not counting the circle for the foot. Cut the end with wire snips. Fold ¼ inch of the top of the leg at a right angle to it. Twist the foot of the leg out in the opposite direction. Make three more legs the same way. When you have all four legs made, use Epoxy and glue the tops of the legs into the middle of each side of the piece of balsa under the table top. Let dry and paint the whole table white. Make two more tables the same way.

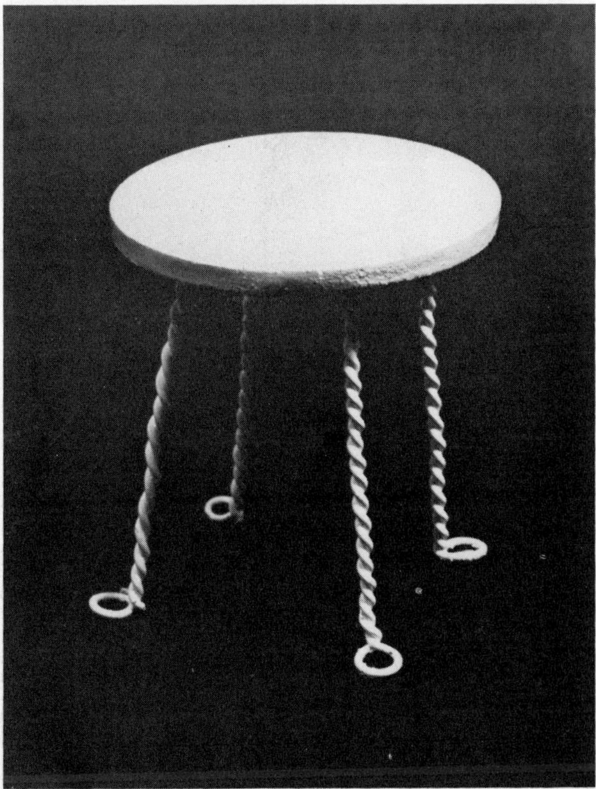

Ice Cream Parlor Table

Without chairs, a place of business could have take-out orders only. Without chairs the customers could not sit down and socialize and spend a few hours. Without chairs there would not be as much business, since a settled customer is more likely to order a second time. For the confectionery, there are two chairs for every table. By making the tables slightly larger, you could have four chairs around them, but this would crowd the eating area.

For each of the six chairs, you will need ⅛-inch-thick basswood for the seats. Using the power saw attachment that makes circles, make six seats 1⅛ inch in diameter. Fill the center holes with plastic Wood Dough. Using ⅛ inch balsa wood, cut six squares, each ⅝ inch square. Glue to the bottoms of the seats. Using the plumber's wire again, make 1¼-inch-long legs for the chairs. You will need at least 4½ inches of the wire for each leg. Fold in half and twist as before

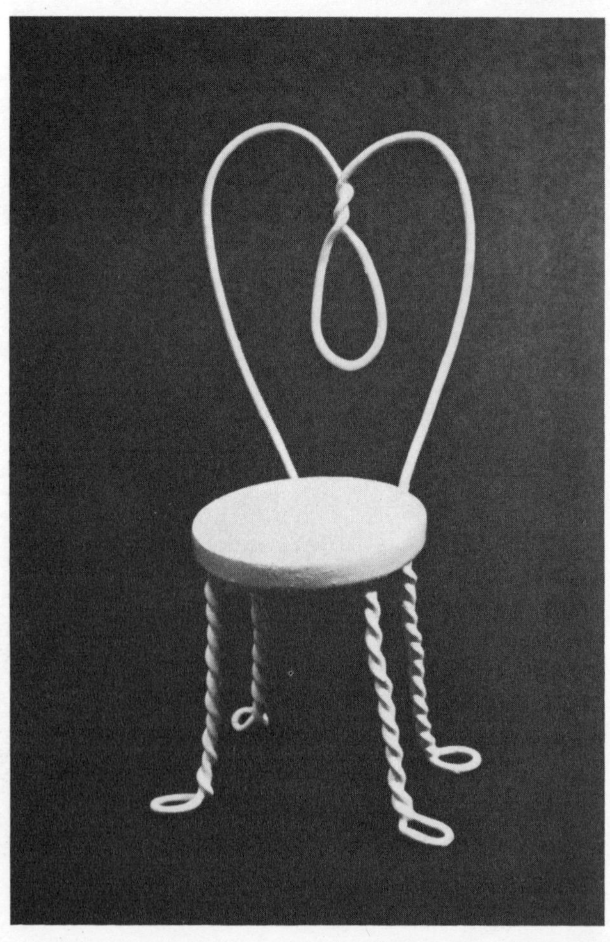

Ice Cream Parlor Chair

until you have legs 1½ inches long, not counting the circular foot. Cut the wire when you are finished and bend ¼ inch of the top of the leg so that you can push it into the balsa wood beneath the chair. With four legs for each chair, glue two into one side and two into the opposite side. For the back of the chair, you will need 5 inches of the wire. Bend ¼ inch at a right angle so that it will fit under the seat and continue to bend and form the chair back as shown, using the handle of a hammer to form the curved tops. The top of the backs should be 1¾ inches above the seat. When you come to the end, fold ¼ inch under again as you did in the beginning and glue these two ends into the balsa beneath the seat. When the glue has dried, paint the chair white, and make five more.

Soda Fountain

It is impossible to imagine a confectionery without a soda fountain. From the mysterious depths of a soda fountain came the rich fruit coverings for sundaes and the sweet syrups and soda water for the sodas that were not yet bottled. The refrigerated units held the fresh fruit for the banana splits and other rich concoctions as well as the ice cream.

For the soda fountain that will fit on top of the long counter, start with a piece of 3/16-inch-thick balsa wood cut to a length of 8½ inches and a width of 2½ inches. For the back of the counter, use ¼-inch-square balsa wood and cut a piece 8½ inches long. Glue along the back of the countertop. For the syrup containers, cut two pieces of the same ¼-inch-square balsa, each 2 inches long. Starting at two opposite corners, make diagonal cuts toward the connecting corner, removing ⅛ inch of that corner so that the piece can sit at an angle on the countertop. Divide these two pieces into four equal sections each by scoring the balsa wood with a pencil and a ruler. Glue to the counter back, leaving 1⅛ inch to the left of the one and 1⅜ inch on the right of the other. Make a drain board for the glasses on the left side of the countertop by scoring 1⅛-inch-long lines from the front to the back of the countertop. Score the rest of the countertop as shown. On the right side of the countertop, cut a hole 1 inch wide by 1½ inches for the sink. Glue a piece of white paper to the bottom. For the handles on the faucets, use two nails. For the spigot and the soda water and syrup spouts, use staple nails with the one side cut shorter. Nail into place and paint the whole countertop silver. Top the syrup and soda water spouts with marblelike beads. Use clear beads on the water faucet handles. Tiny brass nails will serve as handles for lids on

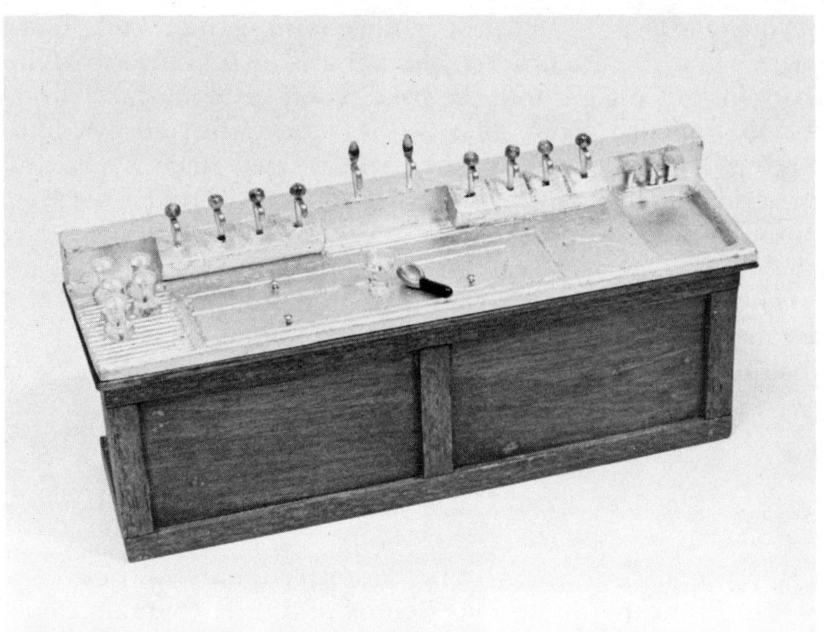

Soda Fountain

the counter surface. Crystal pushpins, with the pins removed, serve as glasses on the drain board, and the ice cream scoop was carved from balsa wood and painted black and silver.

Wall Mirror

A wall mirror in a confectionery served many purposes. It reflected the interior and made the shop look much bigger. It gave the shop an air of elegance. It let the shopkeeper keep an eye on things without turning away from his work. And it certainly must have reassured the young girls on special dates.

For the wall mirror, find a glass shop and ask them to cut you a piece of mirror 7 inches long and 4 inches wide. Glue to a large piece of cardboard. For the sides, cut two pieces of ½-inch-wide balsa wood, each 4 inches long. Glue to the cardboard next to the mirror. For the top and bottom, cut two pieces of ⅜-inch-wide balsa wood, each 8 inches long, and glue into place. For trim on the sides, use the same ⅜-inch-wide balsa and cut into pieces 4 inches long and glue to the middle of the side pieces. When all are dry, cut around the balsa wood frame, leaving the cardboard backing. Stain and varnish the frame and glue to the wall above the soda fountain.

Wall Mirror

Tiffany Lamps

Early twentieth-century sweet shops were often lit with tiffany lamps advertising Cola-Cola, a new fountain specialty. These lamps were made from Ping-Pong balls. I suggest the Halex 3 Star balls because they are thin enough to cut with a pair of cuticle scissors. To make the shade, cut the piece you will use for the top from the ball about ¼ inch beneath the middle line. Cut scallops on the bottom of the shade with the scissors. For the top, cut eight equal peaks on the edge of the small piece. Using a black felt-tipped pen, write Coca-Cola on one side of the shade and the word *drink* on the other. Make the other tiffany designs as shown, working around the words. The top should be edged in black. Make eight sections by drawing lines to the middle from the bases of peaks. For the green and red colors, I recommend acrylics, since I found the felt-tipped pens were not bright enough. Paint the Coca-Cola red, along with every other square in the base. Paint the squares next to the red ones and the word *drink* with green. For the top, paint two opposite sections green, leave a white space, then paint the next two opposite sections red so that you have two red, two green, and four white sections of "stained glass" on the top. Glue the top to the lamp shade. For the light underneath, use a gold, silver, or white ball-shaped button with a circular shank at one

Tiffany Lamps

end. Heat this shank with a match and push it up through the top of the lamp (by melting a small hole). The small gold chain was purchased in a craft shop. Cut a length 3¼ inches long and attach to the shank from the button. For a finishing touch, glue a small piece of gold cord between the shade and top of the lamp. Attach to the beam with a small staple nail, putting one in the eating area and one above the display case.

Piano

Ice cream parlors often offered an added bonus in the way of entertainment when someone played the ever-present piano. Many of these pianos were the player type and could be made to play tunes from metal rolls.

For a piano for the parlor side of the confectionery, use ⅛-inch-thick basswood. Cut two pieces (front and back) 4½ inches wide and 3¾ inches high. Cut two side pieces, each 1⅜ inches wide and 3¾ inches long. Cut a top piece 1½ inches wide and 5 inches long. Cut a bottom piece 1 inch wide and 4½ inches long.

For the compartment that holds the player rolls, cut a hole 1¾ inches long and ¾ inch wide, ½ inch from one of the long edges of the front piece, making sure that it is centered (see photo). For the doors, cut two pieces, each 1 inch wide and 1½ inches long. For the track on which they are to slide, cut two ⅛-inch-wide pieces, each 3½ inches long. Add two small brass nails to the doors for the handles, then place them, handle side down, over the opening. With this guide, glue the two narrow lengths of basswood above and below the doors for them to slide on. On this same piece of wood, on the opposite edge, make a cut ¾ inch long and ¼ inch wide for the foot pedals. Carve three small foot pedals and glue into place, stabilizing them with a piece of basswood ⅛ inch wide and ¾ inch long. Cut two more holes, ¼ inch square, from each of the corners on this same edge to hold the bottom of the legs later on.

Glue the back between the side pieces, then glue the bottom between the three pieces. Glue the front piece on top of the bottom (the sides will overlap), and stabilize with the top of the piano. For trim and support, add a ⅛-inch-wide strip between the front and top piece.

Piano

For the keyboard and front legs, cut the following pieces. Cut one piece 4¼ inches long and 1⅛ inch wide. Cut a second piece 4 inches long and 1⅛ inch wide. Cut a third piece 4 inches long and ⅞ inch wide. Glue the second piece on top of the first, leaving a ⅛-inch margin on either side. Glue the third piece on top of the other two, matching the long, left edge. Along this edge, glue another piece ¼ inch wide and 4 inches long. Using white cardboard, cut a piece ⅝ inches wide and 4 inches long. Mark with piano keys and glue onto the third piece as shown in the picture. For the sides, cut two pieces each 1⅛ inch wide and 1 inch high. Cut two more pieces, 1⅛ inch wide and ⅞ inch high and glue these to each of the larger pieces, leaving a ⅛ inch margin. Sand these two pieces into shape as shown, and glue to the sides of the keyboard. Glue this whole unit to the front of the piano 1¼ inches from the top. For the bottom of the legs, cut four pieces of ⅛-inch-thick basswood into ¼-inch-wide and 1⅛-inch-long pieces. Sand the front edge and glue the pieces into the holes that you had previously cut for them. Using 3/16-inch-thick dowels, cut into pieces, each 1¼ inches long, carve as shown, and glue between the bottom part of the legs and the keyboard. Four small pieces, each ¼ inch square, should be cut and glued beneath the back corners of the piano and the front of the legs. Stain and varnish.

Piano Bench

Piano Bench

For the comfort of the pianist, one should have a bench. Use ⅛ inch basswood and cut a seat 2 inches long and 1 inch wide. For the bottom of the seat, cut two pieces ¼ inch wide and 1⅞ inches long. Cut two more pieces, each ⅞ inch long and ¼ inch wide. Glue the shorter pieces between the longer ones, sand the edges, and glue beneath the piano seat. Cut four pieces of wood ¼ inch long and ⅛ inch square. Glue beneath the seat in each of the four corners. For the four legs, use ¼ inch dowels and cut four legs, each ⅞ inch long. Sand into shape and glue to the bottom of the seat corners. Stain and varnish.

Gumball Machine

Gumball machines have been around for many years, tempting, beguiling, and causing problems for young mothers. They have taken their place in general stores and confectioneries, drug stores and toy shops. They may have had different shapes through the years but their appeal has always been the same.

For this gumball machine, start with a 1-inch-in-diameter dowel cut to a length of ⅞ inch. Make a ⅛-inch-wide groove along the top of one end. The glass dome will fit over this end. This glass dome is really the plastic top of a small toy container that can now be found in such machines. At the opposite end of the dowel, make a small hole ⅜ inch long and ⅛ inch wide. This will be the hole for the gum to drop into. Cut another piece of the 1-inch dowel to a ⅛-inch thickness and glue to this end of the dowel for the bottom of the machine. For the part where you deposit the money, you will need two pieces of ⅛-inch basswood, each ⅝ inch square. Putting sandpaper over the dowel, sand one small square until it fits the curved front. Glue into place above the hole. Cut a small semicircle out of the top of the second piece and then glue over the first one, sanding the side edges until they are rounded. The turning mechanism is made with a ⅜-inch-in-diameter circle of the basswood and a small brass nail. Nail into the front of the small squares. For the stand, use a ⅜-inch dowel. Cut to a length of 1½ inches. Carve as shown. Drill a small ⅜-inch hole in the base of the top and glue the dowel into place. For the base, use ¼ inch basswood (or 2 pieces of ⅛-inch glued together). Cut a piece 1 inch square. Drill a ⅜-inch hole in the middle of the piece. Shape the base

Gumball Machine

as shown. When finished, glue the dowel into place. Paint the machine red. When dry, fill the dome with candy pareils and glue into place.

Cakes

Since a confectionery is also a bakery, there should be a selection of cakes to choose from. These are all made from Repla-Cotta dough. For the chocolate-covered cake and the cherry-topped shortcake, form the dough into a cake shape, no larger than ¾ inch in diameter and ½ inch tall. With a toothpick, make swirls on the top of the chocolate cake. For the cherry topped cake, make a swirled rim, using a piece of dough rolled into a long, thin strip. Place the strip around the top rim of the cake and make indentations with a toothpick. For the lemon square, form the dough into a loaf 1 inch long by ½ inch wide and ½ inch high. Make two ridges around the bottom and the top as you did on the cherry-topped cake. Bake all of these cakes in a 300-degree oven for ten minutes. When they have cooled, use acrylic paints and paint the plain one a chocolate brown (or any icing color). Paint the sides and rims of the other two white. The top of the lemon loaf should be painted yellow. For the cherry-topped cake, glue candy pareils in place and paint them dark red. Display as shown and place on shelves.

Cakes

Bread

Bread

One cannot imagine a bakery without bread, and these two varieties will lend credence to your store. For the French bread, roll the dough into a loaf about 1¼ inches long. Make indentations as shown with a toothpick. The regular loaf is about 1 inch long by ½ inch high. Start with the loaf shape and pull the top down to overlap the sides slightly. After baking, paint both light brown, making the tops slightly darker.

Pastries and Eclairs

A confectionery also served baked goods, and these make excellent individual servings. For the pastries, make ½-inch squares from the dough and fold them into a triangular shape. For the eclairs, make the rounded shells about ⅜ inch long. Trim the top with thin strips, making identations in these strips with a toothpick. Bake as directed. When cool, paint the pastries a golden brown. The eclairs should be painted dark brown and white for the trim.

Cookies

Although mothers still baked a lot at the beginning of this century, there were always special occasions for store-bought cookies. To make these miniature cookies, roll out your dough with a rolling pin and make the individual cookies with the help of the metal eraser holder on the end of a mechanical pencil. Remove the eraser and pull off this metal tube. It is exactly the right size for a cookie cutter, and if the dough gets stuck, you can push it out from the other end with a toothpick. If you don't have a mechanical pencil, you may make small balls and flatten them into the shape of small cookies. After they have been baked, paint some medium brown, some light brown with dark spots for the chocolate chips, some pink, and some green. Glue red and green sugar crystals to the top of the pink and green ones. Display on a large button covered with a doily by gluing the cookies to the doily in an attractive design. Display in the showcase.

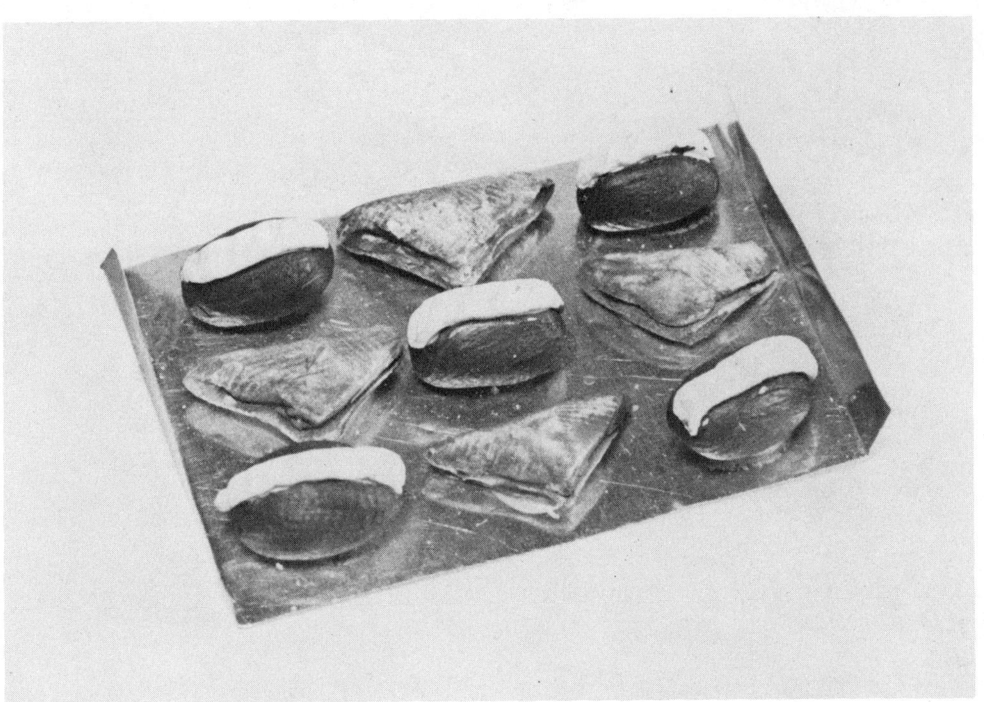

Pastries and Eclairs

Cookies

Doughnuts

Doughnuts

The popularity of doughnuts gave rise to specialty shops later in the twentieth century, but around 1915, doughnuts were still being sold in confectioneries and bakeries. For these doughnuts, use the metal eraser holder you used for the cookies, but start with slightly thicker dough. For the doughnuts that will have holes in them, make holes with round toothpicks. Leave some without holes for the jelly filled variety. When the dough has been baked, paint all the doughnuts golden brown. The glazed doughnuts should be varnished and the chocolate ones should be painted dark brown on the top. Glue sugar to the top of the jelly-filled and brown sugar granules to the tops and sides of the nut-covered doughnuts.

For a display tray, cut a piece of heavy-weight aluminum foil 2¼ inches long by 1¼ inches wide. Fold up the two edges, glue the doughnuts to the tray in rows of three, and place in the showcase.

Danish Rings

Danish rings are just the thing for those who enjoy a sweet bread for either breakfast or brunch. By making two rings, one whole and one sliced, you'll have one to sell to the housewife who wants a breakfast treat and one to serve in pieces to the customers in the confectionery. Make your rings about ⅞ inch in diameter, forming the center hole with the eraser holder you used to make the cookies with. Slice the one *before* baking. When they have been baked, paint them both a medium brown. When the paint is dry, give them a white glaze topping with white paint.

Danish Ring

Wedding Cake

There may not have been as many weddings in 1915 as there are today, but wedding cakes were still in great demand. For this three-tiered wedding cake, make three layers in graduated sizes. The bottom layer should be about the size of a quarter, the middle layer about the size of a nickel and the top layer about the size of a dime. Roll the dough into long strips and decorate the cake sides and rims as shown, creating the design with a toothpick. For the flowers on top of the cake, cut the dough into long pieces ¼ inch wide and roll into the shape of a rose. Place three of these on top of the cake and place three small leaves, made out of the same dough, between them. Use toothpicks for the columns (another variation would be to simply place the layers on top of one another) and bake. Paint the layers and columns white, the roses pink, and the leaves green.

Wedding Cake

Gingerbread

Who can imagine a confectionery without gingerbread houses and gingerbread men for that special childhood occasion? Gingerbread was more common in an age when grandmothers lived in the same household and found time for making such treats, but gingerbread houses are still popular surprises around Christmas.

For the gingerbread men, you will do better if you have a pattern. Make a cardboard gingerbread man no taller than ¾ inches. Lay this pattern on top of rolled out dough and cut out several with the tip of an X-acto knife. The gingerbread house should start with a ¾-inch square. Cut off the top edges to form a roof line and add a roof of thin dough and a door to the front of the house. Bake along with the gingerbread men. When they have cooled, paint the house and the gingerbread men a medium brown. Trim the men with white paint. Paint the roof of the house white as well as outlining the sides and the door. Paint white windows right onto the house and red and white candy canes for decorations.

The gingerbread men stand in a base made from the same Repla-Cotta dough with lines cut into it before baking. Paint the stand beige and glue the gingerbread men in place to display on the shelves.

Gingerbread

Bonbons and Brownies

Somewhere in the history of baking, someone wanted something sweeter than cake but not quite a candy, and brownies were born. For this miniature batch, make a ⅞-inch square of dough and cut into nine pieces, without cutting all the way through the bottom. The bonbons are simply small, round balls of dough that will assume their character when they are painted. After these items are baked, paint the brownies a dark brown and the bonbons pink and light green. Display the brownies on a doily-covered button. The bonbon plate has a small pedestal and was once a button. Painted silver and covered with a doily, it becomes a lovely footed candy dish.

Bonbons and Brownies

Lollipops and Candied Apples

Candied apples have been around since the beginning of this country, since there are records that housewives in the new colonies made varnished apples and the Indians taught them how to use native plants like spearment and peppermint to flavor their candies. For the candied apples, form small balls of the dough and flatten slightly on one end. Use toothpick indentations on the other to make it look more like an apple and insert bits of toothpicks for the sticks. The lollipops are also made with the eraser holder used for the cookies. Insert toothpicks for their sticks as well. Bake and then paint the apples red and the lollipops green and red with yellow and green circle trims. The lollipop holder is made from the dough as well with holes punched into the holder before baking. When it has cooled, paint it beige. Glue the lollipop sticks into the holes. The apples are displayed on a sheet of heavy aluminum. Glue in place to keep them from falling over if jarred.

Box of Candy

Giving a box of candy was more popular around 1915 when girls weren't as diet conscious as they are today. This miniature box started with a piece of cardboard 1 inch long by ½ inch wide. Cut a strip of carcboard 3/16 inch wide by 2½ inches long. Bend to form the rim of the box and glue onto the base. Paint the box gold. Cut white tissue paper 1½ inches long by ⅞ inch wide and glue into place. Cut two pieces of cardboard, each ⅞ inch long by 3/16 inch wide, and paint brown. Glue them into the box as row dividers. For the chocolates, form tiny balls with the dough, bake, and paint dark brown. Cover a couple with aluminum foil. Glue into the rows in the box.

Pies

Pies have always been a popular treat for those who like the taste of fruit with their pastry. For these pies, start with soft-drink bottle caps. For the regular pie, fill with the Repla-Cotta, making a small mound in the middle. With a toothpick, score the edges around the pie and make small identations for the air to escape. Bake and paint golden brown when it has cooled. For pies with lattice work on top, fill the bottle cap almost to the top with the dough. For the edge of the crust, roll the dough into a long, thin strand and put around the top

Lollipops and Candied Apples

Box of Candy

Pies

of the pie, scoring the edges as you did with the other. For the lattice strips, cut four thin strips and place in the middle as shown. Bake to harden the Repla-Cotta. When done, paint the dough golden brown and the inside fruit filling either red for cherry or purple for blueberry.

Sundae, Shake, and Fudge

Every sweet shop needs treats for the customers, and these are enjoyed just as much today as they were in 1910. For the glasses, use clear pushpins. Either pull out or cut off the pins. For the sundae, form a small circular mound of ice cream in the middle of the pushpin from the dough. Paint dark brown. When dry, paint a small white circle for the whipped cream. Glue a tiny circle of dough on top of this and paint red for the cherry. The shake is made with a similar pushpin. Add a flatter but lumpy circle of dough for the shake and paint pink (or light brown for chocolate). The toothpick is the edge of a toothpick painted white and glued into place.

The fudge is also made from Repla-Cotta. Make a small square

Sundae, Shake, and Fudge

and cut into small pieces. Bake. When cool, paint light and dark brown. To display, use a clear button. Glue onto this a round paper doily cut from a larger one, and glue the fudge pieces into place.

Pastry Boxes

Cakes and pies and even gingerbread men would get crushed if they were put into paper bags and carried home. It is for this reason that confectioneries stocked pastry boxes in their bakery section. After putting the baked goods in the boxes, they were often tied with string for safekeeping.

For the cake box, use thin, white cardboard and cut a piece 3 inches long and 1⅞ inch wide, using the following pattern.

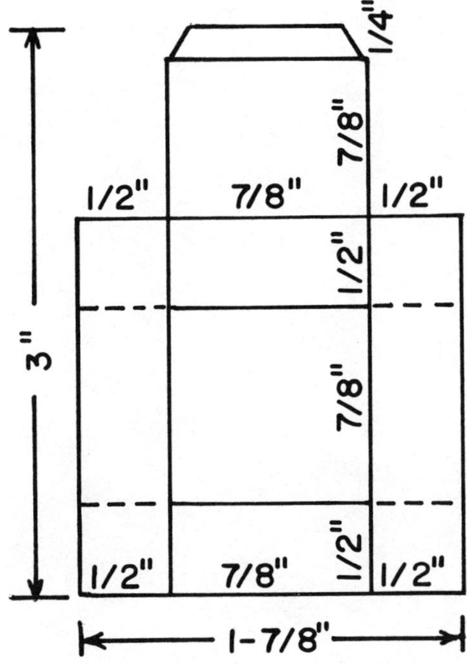

Cut on the dotted lines. Fold and glue the flaps under to form a box shape. A slight variation in the pattern (remember to keep the top and bottom the same and the sides even) will give you different sizes for the different kinds of baked goods.

Pastry Boxes

5

Victorian Millinery

The millinery of the late Victorian period was a source of great enjoyment for women, but the fact remains that men's hats developed long before women's hats.

Ancient Egyptian noblemen wore caps, some with a helmet effect, and ancient Greeks wore the petasos, a small round hat with a flat crown, when traveling. Beaver hats were popular with Englishmen in the fourteenth century, and Charles VIII of France introduced the close-fitting turban that became the forerunner of the woman's turban. Henry VIII of England introduced the sweeping plume, and the Puritan hat became the prototype of the comtemporary sailor hat. George Washington is best remembered in his cocked hat, while Napoleon made the tricorn popular. Both of these hats have been developed into standard shapes for women's hats.

Although Egyptian women of high rank wore headdresses, most women wore veils until the middle ages. The veils were attached to tall, cone-shaped caps during the fourteenth and fifteenth centuries.

Throughout the ages, famous women have influenced the millinery styles of the day. A close-fitting bonnet was worn by Anne of Brittany, while Catherine de Medici and Mary, Queen of Scots, made the widow's mourning bonnets popular. Marie Antoinette and her court ladies wore elaborate headdresses that resembled flower gardens. Empress Eugenie, wife of Napoleon III, made the garden hat stylish, while the simple poke bonnet came into popularity following the French Revolution.

Almost every hat is a modification of the turban, sailor, picture hat, poke bonnet, tricorn, or mourning bonnet. The earliest hats

Millinery

were creations of milliners privately employed by the wealthy. As the popularity of the hat increased, the number of milliners increased, and they eventually opened millineries. By the late Victorian period, it was a well-established business.

The millinery trade had one large drawback. It was a seasonal trade, with most of its business in the spring and fall. The length of a season would determine the profits or losses.

Behind each establishment were the creative hands of the milliners and trimmers who made the hats by hand. If a woman so desired, she could pick out the trimmings and basic shape and have the hat made to suit her needs. The stores also carried other accessories to complement the new hat such as fancy parasols and long white gloves. There might have been a selection of jewelry or shawls as well, but the main emphasis was on the hat styles that changed with every season.

It was an age when people strolled for enjoyment. Women and their fashionable clothes were not hidden behind car doors or flown out of sight in planes. The world seemed to be in less of a hurry then, and women took more time to select accessories that were sure to be noticed.

For the millinery shop, you will need two shelf units, one display counter, a cash register, a telephone, a ladder, and a door from the directions in the first chapter. To make the shop unique, we used walnut instead of oak for the flooring and papered the walls all around. The outfits on the clerk and customer were ordered from Isn't It?, 1618 S. Boulder, Tulsa, Oklahoma 74119, a shop that carries outfits by Nancy Crawford, one of the best mini-seamstresses I have seen. Directions for other items in the shop are given on the following pages.

Dressing Table

The dressing tables in the millineries served two purposes. They gave the customer a comfortable place to try on the new hat she was considering and they also gave the proprietor room to display the latest fashions.

For this dressing table, use ⅛-inch-thick wood. Cut a table top 6 inches long and 2½ inches wide. Cut two pieces for the front and back of the table, each 5⅝ inches long and ⅜ inch wide. Cut two side pieces 2¼ inches long and ⅜ inch wide. Glue the sides between the front and back pieces, beveling the edges to make them form perfect corners. Glue beneath the table top. Cut six legs from ¼-inch-square wood, each 1¾ inches long. Carve as shown and glue in place. Stain and varnish. For the runner, use any fine white material. Cut a piece 8½ inches long and 2½ inches wide. Hem ¼ inch all around. Cut two pieces of fine lace, each 2 inches long, and sew beneath the ends of the cloth.

Make two tables, one for each side of the millinery.

Dressing Table

Dressing Table Bench

A dressing table requires a seat, and this small, padded bench is our answer. For the seat, use ⅛-inch-thick wood and cut into a 1¼-inch-square piece. Top with cotton and cover with velvet, gluing the edges beneath the seat. For the bottom of the seat, cut four sides, each 1 inch long and ¼ inch wide. Bevel the edges, glue together to form a square, and glue beneath the seat. For the legs, use ¼-inch-square wood again and cut four legs, each 1⅛ inch long. Carve as shown and glue into place. Stain and varnish the legs and bottom of the seat. Make four benches, two for each dressing table.

Mirror

Mirrors are a necessity in a millinery. The customer must be able to see if the lines of a hat are becoming as well as stylish. A full, round-faced woman will look good in a hat with a large brim. A thin-faced woman will be able to wear a small hat with a narrow brim. The sharp-featured woman will be sure to reject tailored hats, while an elderly woman will be wise to avoid hats with youthful, straight lines. There are many simple rules, but the customer will want to see for herself and will need a large, wall mirror to do so.

For miniature wall mirrors, buy four 2-inch-by-3-inch oval mirrors in a craft shop. Look for oval, filigree decorative trims and buy four to fit your mirrors. You will also need velvet for the frames. To make the velvet frame, lay the mirror on the back of your piece of velvet and draw around it for a pattern. Cut out the oval. Next, measure the space inside the filigree trim and cut an oval that size from the middle of the velvet. Glue the velvet frame onto the front of the mirror. Using the thickness of the mirror as your width, cut a piece 8¼ inches long. Glue around the edge of the mirror, trimming off any excess. Glue the gold trim in place over the velvet. Make four mirrors and glue two above each dressing table.

Hat Forms

Hats were displayed in many ways in millineries. Some were placed on shelves, others on forms. Even the forms had different shapes. Some were shaped like human heads while others were little more than pedestals of all sizes. Variety gives interest, and a generous supply of both kinds of forms will make your shop more appealing.

Dressing Table Benches

Mirror

For the head-shaped form, use Repla-Cotta. Make your form 1½ inches tall with a 1-inch base. Form the egg-shaped head first, then the neck, and finally the base. Make the face slightly pointed in the front. Bake and paint white.

For the pedestal type of hat form, start with ⅜-inch-thick balsa. Use a nickel for the base pattern and a penny for the top. Trace around the coins and first cut, then sand the circles into shape, rounding off the top edge. From a ⅛-inch-thick dowel, cut a 2-inch piece. Make a hole in the middle of the large circle. Glue one end of the dowel into the base. Cut another shallow hole in the bottom of the smaller circle and glue the other end into this hole. Paint white.

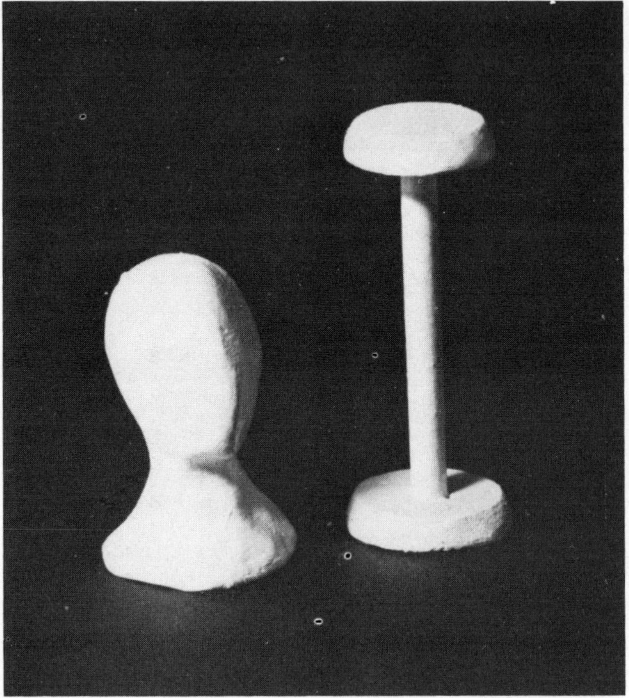

Hat Forms

Shawl Rack

Shawls should be hung to be displayed at best advantage. Hidden in a box, one cannot see the interesting designs on the back nor picture the length of the fringe.

For this shawl rack, use ⅛-inch-thick basswood. Cut two end pieces, each 5 inches high and ½ inch wide with a base 2½ inches long and ½ inch wide. Cut a base support 2½ inches long and ½ inch wide. For the hanger rod, use a ⅛-inch-in-diameter dowel and cut a piece 2¾ inches long. Drill two ⅛-inch-diameter holes in the tops of the side pieces and glue the rod into place. Glue the base support between the bottom of the two sides. Stain and varnish. For the hangers, use thin, brass wire and cut a piece 4½ inches long and twist into the shape of a hanger. Make four and hang on the rod.

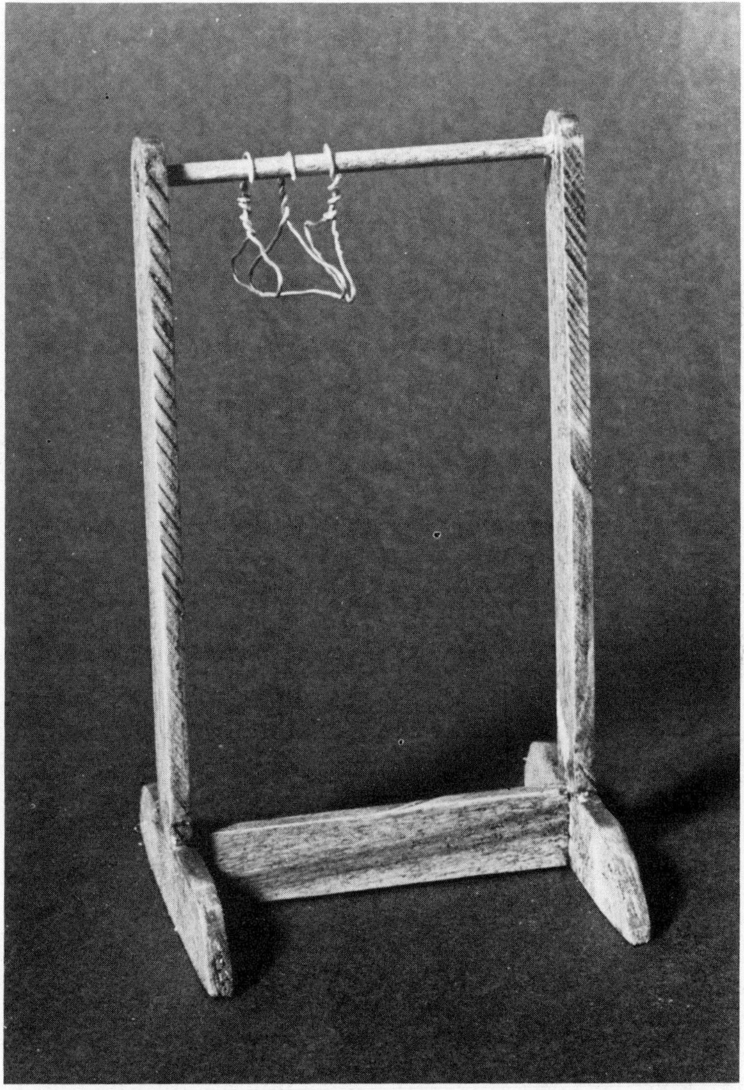

Shawl Rack

Parasol Rack

Parasols should be hung to keep them from touching and wrinkling. This rack makes display a simple matter and shows the parasols off to best advantage.

For this rack, use ⅛-inch-thick basswood and cut a piece 4 inches long and ⅝ inch wide. Drill four ⅛-inch-in-diameter holes in the middle, spaced equal distances apart, and make slits large enough for the parasol handles to pass through from these holes to the right edge of the piece. For the supports, start with two ⅝-inch-square pieces of basswood and curve like a bracket. Glue on either side beneath the shelf. Stain and varnish and slide four parasol handles through the slits and into the holes.

Parasol Rack

Hat Boxes

Hat boxes served a dual purpose. They not only let the customer carry her new hat home without crushing it, but they also served as a storage unit between uses.

For hat boxes in the millinery, you will need small remnants of wallpaper used in the shops or wrapping paper with tiny designs. You may want to cover all the hat boxes with the same paper that you used on the walls. Shops used to do this so that people would automatically know where the purchase was made.

Glue the paper you have chosen to large index cards or construction paper. While it is drying, cut the following patterns. For a round hat box, make two circles, one 1 inch in diameter for the bottom of the box, and the other 1⅛ inch in diameter for the top. Cut a side pattern 3½ inches long and 1 inch wide. Cut a band for the top of the box 3⅝ inches long and ¼ inch wide. Using this pattern, cut the pieces from the paper you chose. Glue the side to the bottom of the box (overlapping the side) and the band to the top. Hold until dry. Glue narrow velvet ribbon, satin ribbon, or tiny lace to the band and the bottom edge of the box.

For an oval hat box, cut a bottom that is 1 inch wide and 1⅜ inches long. Cut a top that is 1 inch wide and 1½ inches long. The side should be 4 inches long and 1 inch wide. The top band should be 4⅛ inches long and ¼ inch wide. Proceed as before.

Larger and smaller boxes may be made by changing the dimensions slightly.

Hat Boxes

Felt Hat

Felt hats have been manufactured since the dawn of civilized man. Some say it was originated by St. Clement, and his feast day, the twenty-third of November, used to be the festival day for the trade. Others claim that the petasos, a wide-brimmed hat worn by ancient Greek men on their travels, closely resembled modern felt hats. Whatever we choose to believe, the felt hat has unique stretching properites, which makes it fun to work with.

For this wide-brimmed Victorian hat, start with a circle of felt 2 inches in diameter. Using the tall hat form as a frame, center the piece of felt and fold down the sides over the top of the form. Glue a length of narrow ribbon around the hat crown to secure this shape and let the wide brim spring back into place. Decorate with flowers and feathers.

Felt Hat

Wide-Brimmed Hats

Wide-brimmed hats were popular with the Victorian women and went well with their long skirts. The hats were often worn tilted to one side and many flowers and feathers adorned their brims.

For this wide-brimmed hat, use suedecloth. Cut a 1¾-inch-in-diameter brim with a ⅝-inch-diameter hole in the middle. To make the brim curved, cut through the brim and overlap it slightly and glue into place. Using a nickel for a pattern, cut the circle for the crown. For the side of the crown, cut a piece of suedecloth ⅜ inch wide and 3 inches long. Glue the side around the top of the crown, holding it until it dries. Turn the crown over and glue onto the large brim. When it has dried, turn the back of the brim up to touch the crown and glue into place. Trim the hat with flowers and feathers.

Wide-Brimmed Hats

Narrow-Brimmed Hat

Even in the Victorian era, women sought to be improved by just the right hat. This meant finding the right shape for their features as well as the right trimmings. Many women did not look good in the large-brimmed hats and needed the smaller brim to accentuate certain features. There were numerous styles available.

For this narrow-brimmed hat, use the suedecloth again. Cut a brim 1½ inches in diameter with a ⅝-inch hole in the middle. Slit one side and overlap the brim for a slight curve. Use the nickel for the pattern for the top of the crown and make the side from a piece of material ¼ inch wide and 3 inches long. Glue the side around the top of the crown and hold until dry. Then glue the crown onto the brim. For a different trim, use ¾-inch-wide lace. Cut a piece 8 inches long and fold in half. Sew a gathering stitch through both of the finished edges and pull the threads until the lace fits around the side of the crown of the hat. Sew into place. For a final touch, glue a small, filigree flower in the middle of the front.

Narrow-Brimmed Hat

Bonnets

Babies and grandmothers wore bonnets. Women of certain religious sects wore bonnets. Many brides chose the bonnet for a headpiece for their wedding veil. The bonnet seemed to stand for innocence, purity, and dignity. Whatever the reason for its popularity, the bonnet came into vogue as a fashionable headdress in the gay nineties.

To make this bonnet, you will need thin, white cardboard, a 4-inch length of 2-inch-wide satin ribbon, narrow lace for the brim, and some velvet ribbon for the trim. Use the following pattern and cut the bonnet brim and crown from the ribbon, cutting two brims and two crowns if you want to line the bonnet. Using the same pattern, cut one brim and one crown from the cardboard.

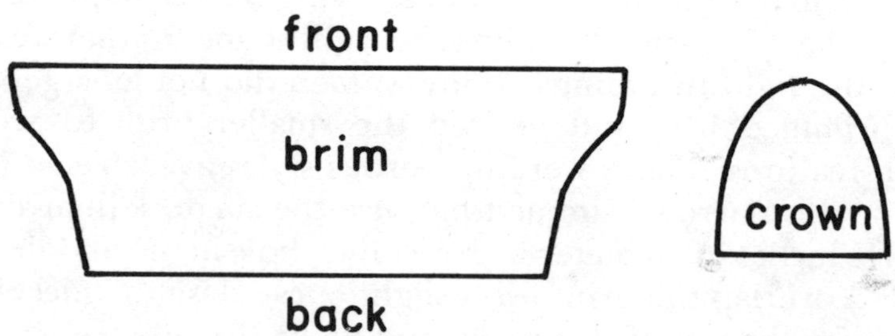

Glue the ribbon to both sides of the cardboard brim and crown. Glue the lace to the front edge of the bonnet brim, letting a little overlap. When this is dry, coat the edge of the crown with a little glue and fold the back edge of the brim over the crown, holding it in place until it is dry. For the trim, glue narrow velvet ribbon across the bonnet as

Bonnet

shown. Cut this width in half (or use suedecloth, which will not ravel) and glue into place for the ties. You may also wish to add flowers or bows to your bonnet. Make several in different colors.

Straw Hats

Straw hats used to be made by peasant women in France in the thirteenth century and sold on the regular market days. The first straw hat made in America was made in 1799 by Miss Betty Metcalf in Dedham, Massachusetts. She made the hat from 7-strand oat straw she wove herself. In 1840, looms were adapted to straw-braiding and straw hats no longer had to be braided by hand, although the expensive ones were still handwoven in Victorian times.

For these miniature straw hats, we used Coats and Clark's six-strand gold floss. For the frames, use thin, white cardboard. For the small sailor hat, cut a circle 1¼ inches in diameter. The top of the crown should be ¾ inch in diameter and the sides of the crown shoud be ¼ inch wide and 3 inches long. Twist the side piece around a pencil to make it curved and then glue around the edge of the top of the crown. Cut a ⅝-inch circle from the center of the brim. Glue the crown on top of the brim. Starting in the middle of the crown, glue the floss onto the hat one row at a time. Stop at the edge of the crown and start a new row for the side. Then start a new row when you get to the brim. Glue the floss to the underside of the hat as well. Trim with a ribbon as shown.

For the wide-brimmed straw hat, make the brim 1¾ inches wide. Make the crown as you did for the smaller straw hat and glue to the large brim after you have cut out the center hole. Attach the floss as before and trim with ribbons and flowers.

You may also purchase commercial kits for making miniature straw hats from dealers. These hats are most attractive and will give variety to your shop.

Jewelry

The Victorian age was one of frills and fancy decorations. The exteriors of homes had gingerbreading and the furnishings were elaborately carved. Fashions were also elaborate and jewelry was very popular. A millinery could easily have carried a line of jewelry to complement the hats.

For miniature jewelry, you will need display stands. Cut pieces of cardboard 1 inch high by ⅞ inch wide and cover with felt or suede. Cut a stand for the back ¼ inch wide and ⅝ inch long and bend under ⅛ inch. Glue this tab to the back of the display so that it will stand up on the shelf. For pearls, look for tiny strands of pearls in the trim department of your fabric shop. A piece 2¼ inches long will make a single strand. Shape and glue to the velvet or suede (it will not stick to thinner fabrics). Glue a second strand inside the first for a double row of pearls. For earrings, glue a single pearl on either side of the necklace. Colored necklaces may be made from tiny beads strung together and glued on as you did the pearls. Pins are small beads surrounded by the strand of pearls. Slightly larger, round, flat beads with marbled designs will also work when painted gold around the edges and glued to the velvet. You may also find interesting miniature pins among old, tiny buttons or make your own with pictures glued to baby buttons. Vary your display with different-sized stands using fabrics of different colors.

Ribbon Rack

Loose ribbons were often sold in millineries. They might have been bought for a hair ribbon for a daughter or used as a trim on a hat. Fixed as bows, they might have trimmed packages or blouses.

Straw Hats

Jewelry

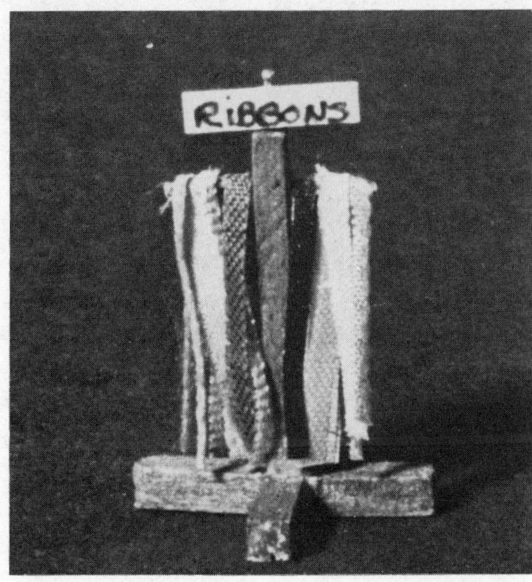

Ribbon Rack

There were many possibilities when the selection was varied.

For a ribbon rack for the counter top, use ⅛-inch-square balsa. Cut a center piece 1⅛ inch long. Cut one base piece ⅞ inch long and two shorter ones ⅜ inch long. Glue the two shorter pieces on either side of the center of the larger base piece. Carve a small square hole in the middle of this piece for the center piece to go into. To hold the ribbons, use two small brad nails on opposite sides of the center piece near the top. Glue the bottom of this piece into the middle of the base. Stain and varnish. For ribbons, cut narrow lengths of ribbon and material and glue onto the brads. As a final touch, write the word *ribbons* on a small piece of white paper. Glue this sign to a brad and push the bottom of the brad into the top of the center piece.

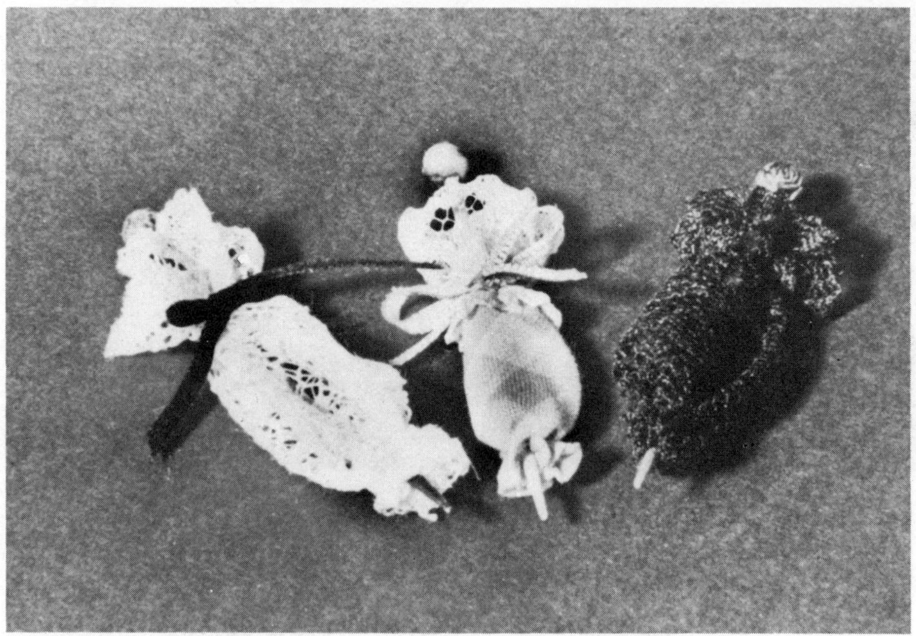

Parasols

Parasol

Parasols were indispensible for strolling, not because they kept off the rain but because they kept off the sun. A deep tan was representative of the lower classes who had to work outside for a living, whereas a lady of means treasured and pampered a pale, delicate complexion.

For lace parasols, start with round toothpicks. Paint them black, white, and gold. Find small beads and glue to one end for the handles. For the parasols, use 2-inch-wide lace (or lace and material combinations), and cut into 2½-inch lengths. Seam the two short edges together. Run a gathering stitch ¼-inch from one edge. Put the toothpick through the circle of lace and pull the gathered edge until the lace fits tightly around the pointed end of the toothpick. Wrap the thread around the gathers, tie, and cut. Run another row of gathering stitches ½ inch from the other edge of the lace and tighten, wrap and knot as before. For a finishing touch, you may want to add a small bow in a color to complement the color in your lace and material combination or to match your handle if you are using plain-colored lace.

Fans and Gloves

Modesty was a virtue of the dignified Victorian woman. She hid her smiles behind a fan and her hands beneath long gloves.

For miniature fans, look in the lace department at your local fabric shop. Many laces have the small fan pattern right in them while others may have a partial fan that could be cut to fit. Glue to small cardboard fan shapes.

For the gloves, I used white mending tape because it did not ravel. Cut two pieces, each 1 inch long and ¾ inch wide. Fold each in half lengthwise, iron together, then cut the glove shape with fingers as shown. Add thumbs from pieces ⅜ inch long and ¼ inch wide. Fold in

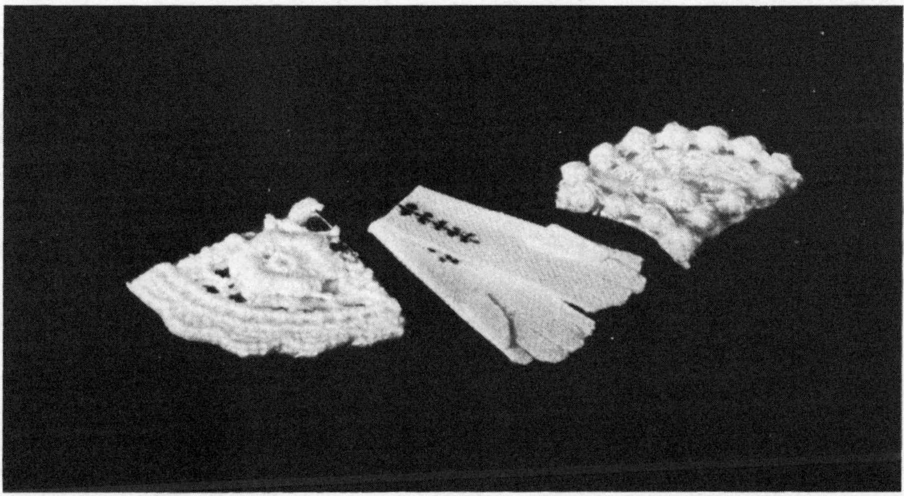

Fans and Gloves

half, iron, and cut into shape as shown. Glue to the gloves. Use a fine brush and black paint for the slit and tiny buttons at the wrist. Make several pair and place in long narrow boxes in the display counter. You may also want to make some in different colors and even some from thin leather or kid.

Flowers and Feathers

Many Victorian millineries offered a unique service in letting their customers choose the forms and trims for their hats. Some women simply wanted new accessories to retrim old hats. Flowers and feathers were subject to change with the seasons and fashions. Some flowers might have been used singly, others in bunches, and some petals would also have been used to make crowns. Large sprays of feather wings might be used one season while ponpons or small motifs might have been popular the next season. To keep the women in style, the millineries stocked a varied supply of many different trims.

To make the boxes for the flowers and feathers, use thin white cardboard and cut a piece 2 inches long and 1½ inches wide as shown.

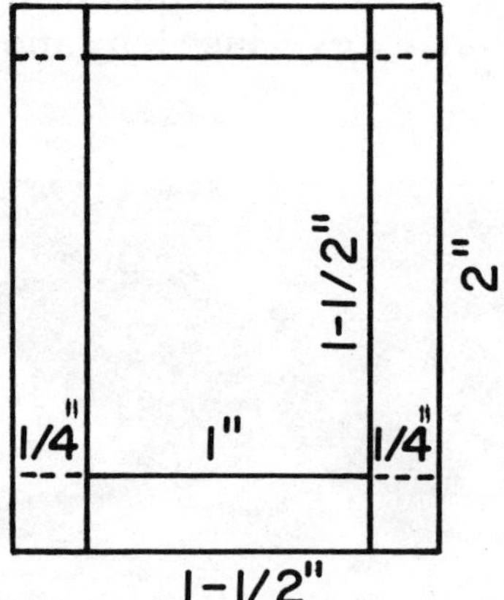

Cut on the dotted lines. Write the word *flowers* or *feathers* on one narrow edge of each box form. Turn the sides up (with the word on the outside) and glue the flaps under, making a box. Fill with tiny flowers and feathers and put on a shelf in the display counter.

Flowers and Feathers

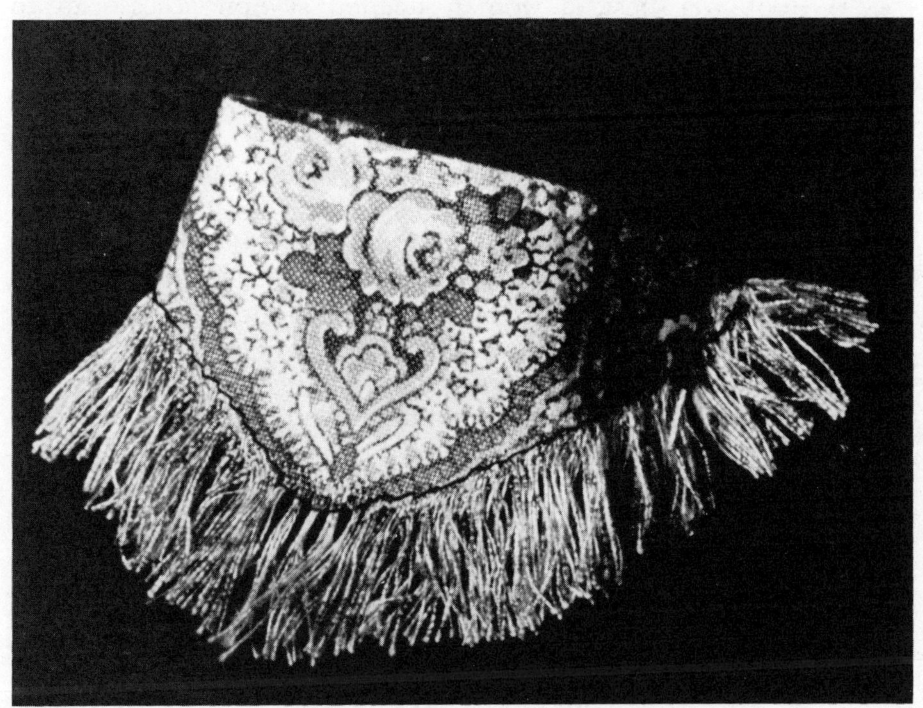

Shawl

Shawl

Shawls were popular with the Victorian woman. In fact, anything with a flowing effect was popular. There were capes and collarettes, and even the mackintosh had a caped effect. Since the cape was an accessory for strolling, it might very easily have been sold in a millinery.

For this shawl, find a piece of material that has a design suitable for a miniature shawl. Cut a triangular piece 5½ inches long at the top and 4 inches long on each of the two bottom edges. Turn the long edge under ¼ inch and hem. For the raveled effect, draw a line ¾ inch from the edge all the way around the two bottom sides.Stitch along this line. Pull the cross threads starting at the bottom, but only pull them to the stitching on the sides.

If you can crochet, you might want to try several of these tiny shawls to hang beside the others on the rack.

Purse and Stockings

To look her best, a woman needed several accessories to complete her ensemble. She needed stockings to go with the new shoe styles and she needed a purse in which to carry her comb and money. This rule is still in effect, but the styles were quite different during the Victorian era.

To make the drawstring purse, use 1-inch-wide black-beaded trim found in the fabric store. Cut a piece 2 inches long. Line with black material, then hem the two short edges. Fold in half, with the outside turned in, and sew the two sides together. Turn back to the right side. Using double thread, run a gathering stitch around the top from each of the sides, ending up with two ends on each side. Leave a 1-inch allowance on the ends and knot them together on each side. Fill the purse with cotton to give it a bulky body that will stand on a shelf, and draw the strings.

For the stocking boxes, use white index cards. For each top, cut pieces 1 inch wide and ¾ inch long, using the pattern below.

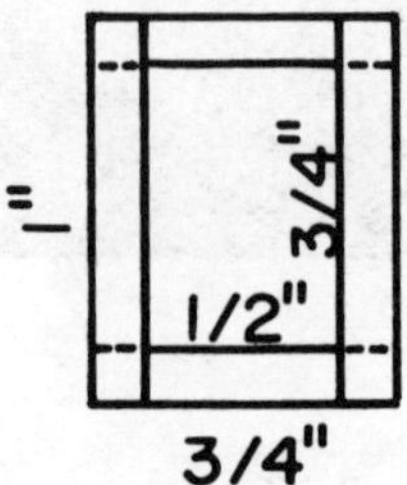

Cut on the dotted lines. Write the word *stockings* on one of the shorter edges. Next, fold up the edges, gluing the tabs into place to form a box. Make two bottoms for the boxes, using the same pattern minus $^{1}/_{16}$ inch all around. Stack the boxes and glue a small flower pattern on the top one.

Purse and Stockings

6

1861 One-Room Schoolhouse

In 1647 a law was passed in Massachusetts that made public schools mandatory, and one-room district schoolhouses came into being. They developed and spread across the rural areas of the United States. Many of these schools are still standing, and fine examples may be seen in re-created villages such as Meadowcroft Village in Avella, Pennsylvania, or Old Sturbridge Village in Sturbridge, Massachusetts. There is also an excellent example in the Smithsonian. Some of the schools are still being used in rural areas by the Amish and other religious sects.

By today's standards, the one-room schoolhouse was very primitive. The schoolroom was small, made for passive listening rather than active work. There was no place for groups to withdraw to work together. The cross lighting from windows on opposite walls was a strain on the children's eyes. There was little or no ventilation to remove the stale air, especially in winter when the stove added its smoky pollution to the chalkdust and cold germs. The romantic double desk was in fact the cause of many round shouldered adults. Sanitation was often lacking since the drinking well was rarely cleaned and the outbuildings were left untended.

Discipline was strict and the dreaded dunce stool was always waiting for those who didn't have time to do their homework and couldn't answer the questions. Needless to say, there were neither children's clubs nor parent conferences. Although there were six to eight classes in each school, some grades only had one or two pupils, hardly a good basis for creative competition.

One-Room Schoolhouse

The teacher was truly a remarkable person. Along with long, muddy walks to school, cold lunches, and heavy janitorial work, he or she had to endure the nervous strain of managing twenty-five to thirty daily recitations and the general direction of an ungraded school. The teacher had to be, in addition to a scholar, an artist, a carpenter, a musician, and a gardener. He had to be able to fix a smoky stove, bandage wounds, pull teeth, start fires, and fix a rattling window—all for forty to fifty dollars a month.

Yet out of these schoolhouses, with their spelling bees and lessons by rote, came some of our country's greatest poets, statesmen, writers, and scientists. For many, the one-room schoolhouse, with all its faults and virtues, was the key to a lifetime of great contributions.

For our schoolhouse, you will need, in addition to the basic box with its walls painted white, a pot-bellied stove, woodbox, and school clock described in the general store chapter. You will also need a door as described in the first chapter. It will be glued to the middle of the wall on the left. For the paneling, use ⅜-inch-wide balsa wood cut to 3-inch lengths. Glue into place, leaving room for the door. On the two walls with windows, make the paneling 2¾ inches high beneath the windows to allow for the frame. The chair rail is made from ⅛-inch-square balsa wood and the baseboard is made from ¼-inch-wide balsa. You may stain the balsa either before or after gluing into place. Varnish to bring out the highlights of the wood. On a piece of white matting board 20 inches long and 1⅛ inches high, print the large and small letters of the alphabet, using a Leroy lettering set. Glue this strip to the wall facing you and you are ready to fill your schoolroom with the pieces found on the following pages.

Blackboard

There were not as many blackboards in one-room schoolhouses as there are in modern schools, but they were usually filled with every child's need. On a single blackboard, the teacher found space to challenge all of his students. There might have been sentences to be copied by second graders and division problems for fourth graders. A corner might have held a geometric figure for some of the older students, and there was always room to note the ones who had misbehaved and would have to remain after school.

For the miniature blackboard, use black matting board. Cut a piece 4 inches wide by 3½ inches high. Frame on the top and sides with 3/16-inch-wide balsa. For the bottom ledge, use balsa that is ⅛-inch square so that it will protrude slightly. Stain and varnish the balsa. For the writing, use white ink and a fine-tipped pen. The chalk was made from the ends of toothpicks painted white and glued into place. Glue the completed blackboard to the wall on the left of the door.

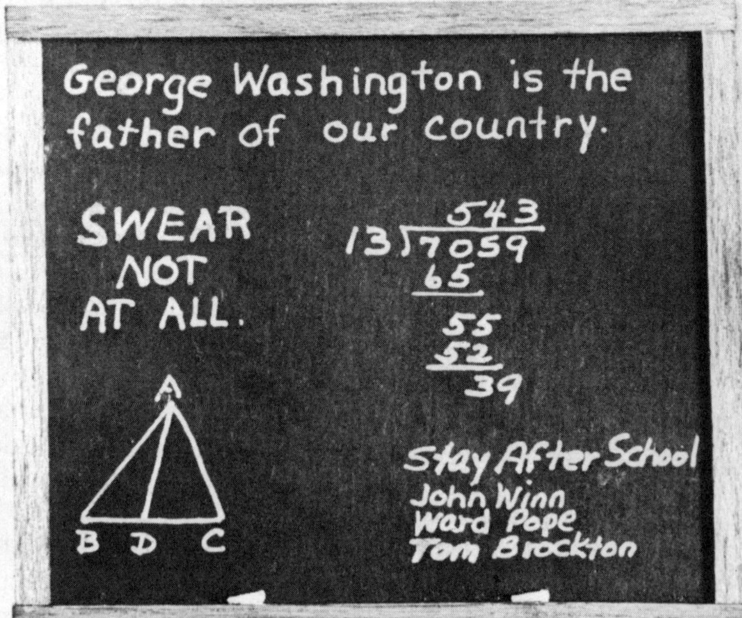

Blackboard

Every one-room schoolhouse had wall maps to help with geography and history lessons. These maps are easily found in miniature in history books, but take into account the date of the school. An 1860 schoolhouse would not have a modern map showing many of the western cities that came into being after that date. Our map came from a book entitled *History of Europe 1500-1848* by Henry Littlefield. The map showing the routes of the Spanish explorers was Xeroxed and then colored with red, yellow, and blue felt tip pens.

For the wall-sized map, cut the map into a piece 4 inches wide by 3½ inches high. Glue to a piece of thin cardboard. Cut two pieces of ⅛ inch balsa wood into 4-inch lengths. Stain fruitwood and glue to the top and bottom of the map. Glue the finished map to the wall on the right side of the door.

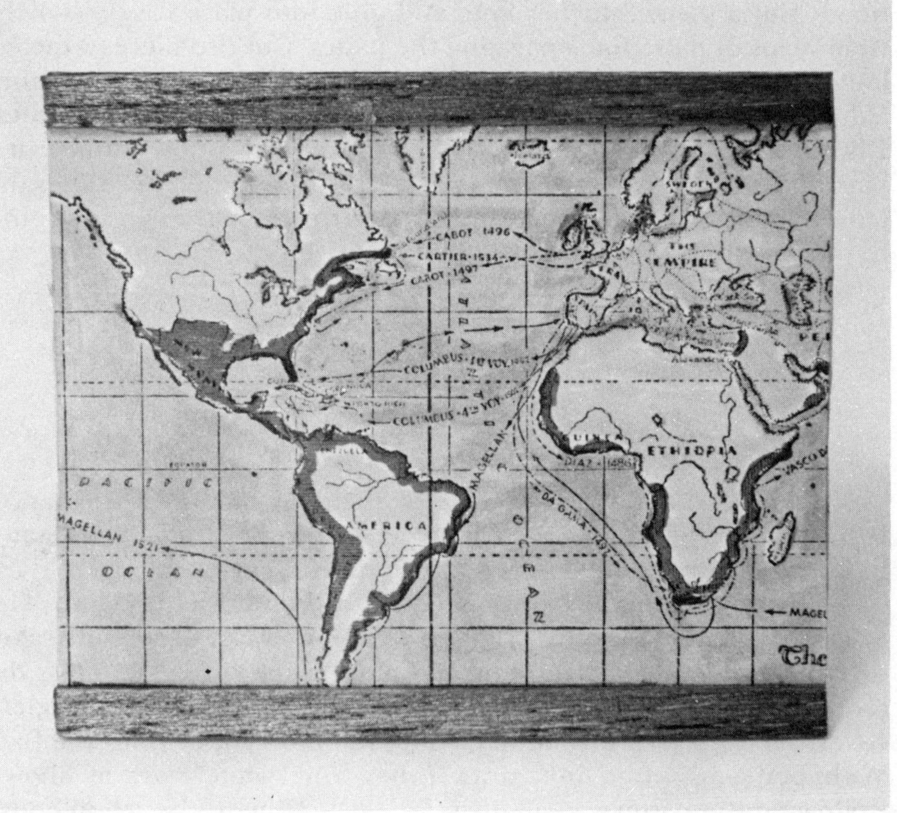

Wall Map

Windows

Like doors, windows give a box room dimension, especially if there are several covering a continuous scene. As room creator, you determine the time of year and the type of weather. It could be fall with the leaves turning or spring with new flowers blooming, or as we decided, winter with snow blanketing the ground.

After you have decided on your season, go to the nearest craft shop or art shop and find a print large enough to have three scenes cut from it, each being 3 inches wide and 5¼ inches high. It will be better if you can leave space between the cut sections since that will make it look more natural. Glue the print to cardboard. When dry, draw your picture sections and cut them out. Use clear acetate for the window pane, cutting pieces the same size and gluing to the pictures around the edges.

For the window frame, use 3/16-inch-wide balsa. Cut two pieces 5¼ inches long and two pieces 3 inches long. Glue around the picture as shown. For the divider in the middle, use ⅛-inch-square balsa wood. Cut a piece 3 inches long and glue into place. Use 1/16-inch-wide strips of balsa for separating the panes. Cut two pieces 3 inches long and eight pieces 1⅛ inches long. Glue as shown. For the bottom ledge, cut a piece of the 3/16-inch-wide balsa to a length of 3¾ inches. Glue to the bottom of the window. To finish the window frame, cut a piece of this same width to a length of 3 6/16 inches and glue under the ledge. Stain and varnish the frame. When dry, glue the windows onto the walls within the spaces left in the paneling.

Flag

Every schoolhouse had a flag for the daily pledge of allegiance. In 1861, on the brink of the Civil War, the flag of the United States had thirty-four stars to represent the states.

This flag was made from a party favor found in a card shop. The original favor had a toothpick glued behind it (for insertion into cakes or cupcakes) and fifty stars on the blue background. Remove the toothpick and cut a piece of blue construction paper large enough to cover the blue area on the flag. Glue the blue paper onto the flag. With pen and white ink, draw thirty-four white stars as shown (following the pattern in an encyclopedia). Glue to the schoolhouse wall above the door.

Windows

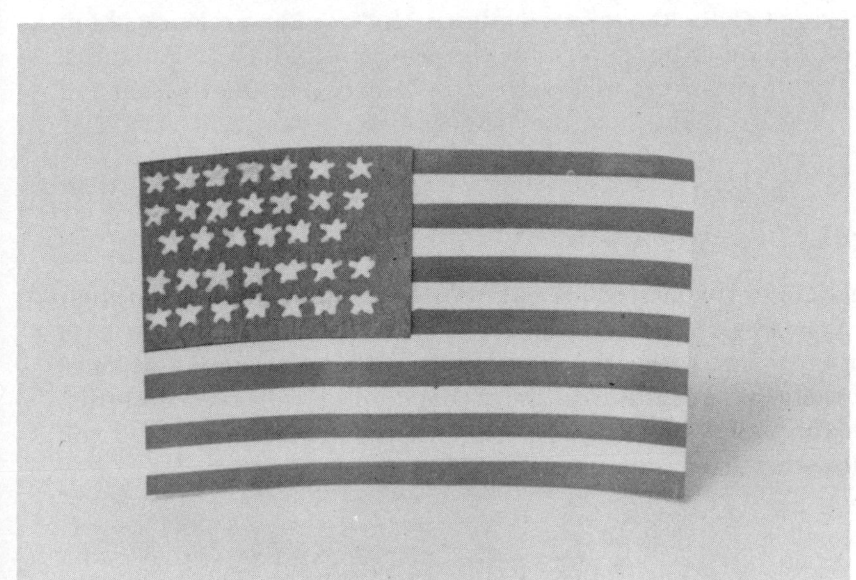

Flag

Teacher's Desk

Early schoolhouses contained only the bare necessities, and this was often reflected in the design of the teacher's desk. Often as not, they were handmade and little more than a table for the teacher to use when grading papers.

This desk, similar to the one at the schoolhouse in the Smithsonian, is made from ⅛-inch-thick basswood. For the front, cut a piece 3 inches wide by 2½ inches high. Cut two side pieces, each 2 inches wide by 2½ inches high. Bevel the edges (make 45-degree diagonal cuts in them) and glue the front to the sides. For the top, cut a piece 3¼ inches long by 2¼ inches wide. Glue on top of the three sides, leaving a ⅛-inch ledge all around. For the bottom, finish off with ¼-inch-wide strips that are 1/16-inch-thick. Cut two pieces, each 2 1/16 inches, for the sides and one piece 3⅛ inches for the front. Bevel the connecting edges and glue to the base of the desk. Stain and varnish.

Teacher's Chair

Like the desk, the teacher's chair was often handmade and crude by today's standards. The teacher could neither swivel nor lounge, but then he or she hardly had the time to even sit during the busy routine of the small schoolhouse.

For the chair, start with ⅛-inch-thick basswood. Cut a back 3 inches high by 2 inches wide. Make the seat 1⅞ inches wide by 1 inch deep. The two legs should be 1⅜ inches high by 1 inch wide at the top and tapered to ¾ inch wide at the bottom. Glue the legs to the back, remembering to keep the tapered edge in the front and leaving about ⅛-inch margin on either side. Glue the seat on top of the legs against the back. You may add ⅛-inch-wide strips of wood under the seat and inside the legs to make sure they stay in place. Stain and varnish.

Teacher's Desk Accessories

Teachers in the late 1800s did not need as many things on their desks as teachers do today. There was no need for an appointment book for meetings with other teachers, and papers were few since much of the work was done on slates that could be checked and then wiped clean. A copy of each McGuffey reader was necessary and you may follow the directions given later for these.

Teacher's Desk

Teacher's Chair

Teacher's Desk Accessories

The teachers also used pointers so that students could follow them at the blackboard, and this one started as a 2¾-inch length of balsa wood that was 3/16-inch square. Using medium sandpaper, sand into the shape of a pointer. Paint black.

Use ⅜-inch-square balsa wood for the bell and start with a piece 2⅞ inches long. Sand into shape as you did the pointer, starting with the shape of the bell and then forming the handle. Paint the bell gold and the handle black.

The teacher's pen is a bead cap topped with a crystal bead. The pen is the pin you pulled out of the crystal pushpins in the confectionery. Simply glue into the hole in the bead at an angle.

For personal touches, you may want to add a red apple or a pair of glasses (general store chapter) on top of the desk. You may also add a pipe made from Repla-Cotta, baked for hardness and then painted.

Front Desk

The front desk was different from the others in that it did not have a front seat. Some schoolhouses simply used the smallest desk with a seat for the front and let the first graders sit there, but in this schoolhouse, there is a separate desk that marks the front of the row.

You will need two of these front desks. Use ⅛-inch-thick basswood. Cut two desk tops, each 4 inches long by 1¼ inches wide. For the front, cut two pieces 4 inches long by 1¾ inches wide. Cut four side pieces 1½ inches high with the one side tapered from 1⅛ inches at the top to ⅞ inch at the bottom. Leaving an edge of ⅛ inch on the top, glue the top to the front. Leaving a ⅛-inch margin on the sides and beneath the top, glue the sides to the front and top. You may use lengths of square balsa wood beneath to hold it in place. For shelves under the desks cut two pieces of ⅛-inch-thick balsa wood 3½ inches long by ⅝ inch wide. Glue between the sides about ⅜ inch beneath the top of the desk. Stain and varnish the two desks.

Front Desk

Early schoolrooms had wooden desks in graduated sizes to accommodate the children in various classes. Unfortunately, these desks did not fit everyone. Bad posture habits were formed as small children swung their legs when they were unable to touch the floor and older students often sat cramped in seats too small for them. It was an era that did not place great emphasis on a child's comfort, and it would be years before the desks with adjustable seats were adopted.

For the smallest of the three desks pictured (the one that goes behind the front desk), you will need ⅛-inch-thick basswood. There should be two of each of these desks (six in all). For the smallest, cut two seat pieces 4 inches long by 13/16 inch wide. The backs of the seat should be 4 inches long by 1 inch wide. The tops of the desks are 4 inches long by 1¼ inches wide. The sides are cut from a piece 1¾ inches long and 2 inches wide. Cut four sides as shown in the drawing:

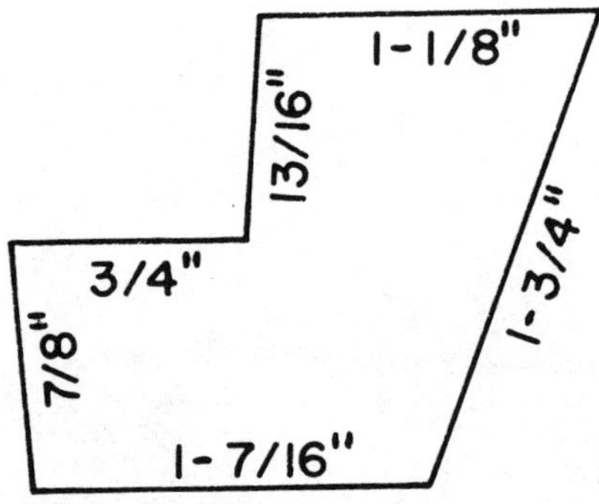

Leaving a ⅛-inch overlap on each side, glue the seat into place on the sides, then the seat backs and finally the desk tops as shown in the photo. Small square strips of wood may be glued beneath the desks at the seams to hold the pieces in place. For the shelves beneath the desks, cut two pieces, each ¾ inch wide by 3½ inches long, and glue in place ⅜ inch beneath the desk top.

For the middle-sized desks, use the same ⅛-inch-thick basswood. Cut two seat pieces 4 inches long by ⅞ inch wide. The backs of the seats should be 4 inches long by 1¼ inch high. The desk tops should be 4 inches long by 1⅜ inches wide. Cut four side pieces as shown.

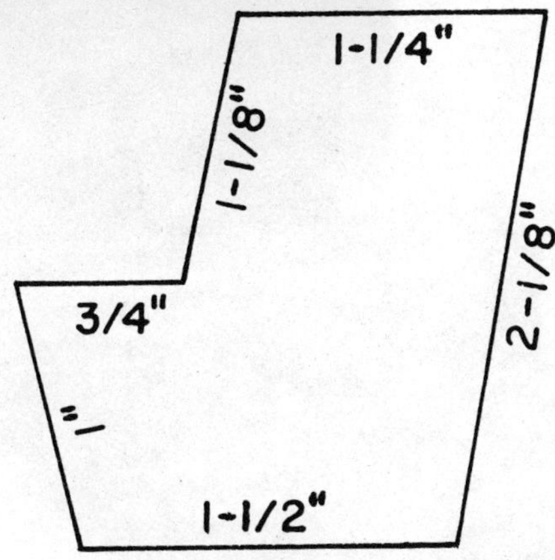

Glue together as you did the other desks. For the shelves inside the desks, cut two pieces, each 3½ inches long by ⅞ inch wide, and glue into place.

For the largest desks, cut two desk seats 4 inches long by 1 inch wide. The seat backs should be 4 inches long by 1½ inches wide. The desk tops should also be 4 inches long by 1½ inches wide. For the four sides, use the following pattern:

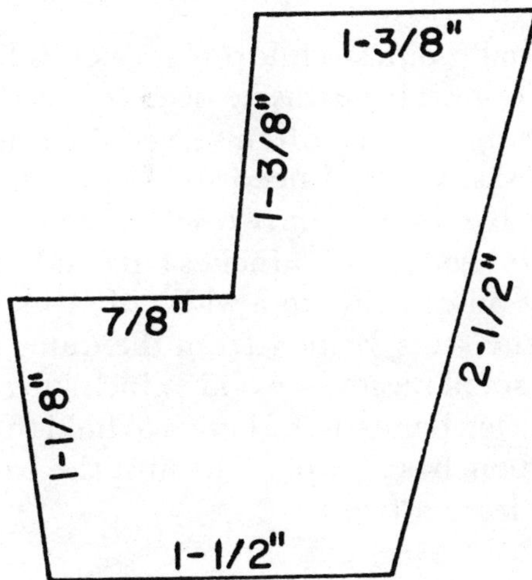

The inner shelves should be 3½ inches long and ⅞ inch wide. Assemble as before.

When the glue has dried, stain and varnish the desks.

School Desks

Rear Bench

The tallest and usually oldest children sat behind the biggest desks in the rear of the room. There was no need for yet another desk behind these seats so a single bench often served the purpose. Since we have two rows of desks, you will need two benches.

Using ⅛-inch-thick basswood, cut two seats, each 4 inches long and 1 inch wide. Cut four legs, each 1⅜ inches long and 1 inch wide at the top but tapering off on one side to a width of ¾-inch across the bottom. Glue beneath the seats ¼ inch from the outer edge of the benches. You may glue small pieces of wood ¾ inch long and ⅛ inch wide on either side of the leg beneath the bench to hold the leg secure. Stain and varnish both benches and place against the back wall with the tapered side of the legs in front.

Bookshelf

With limited floor space in the small schoolhouses, storage shelves were often fastened to the walls. There was always a need for extra bookshelves to house song books and volumes of poems for

Rear Bench

Bookshelf

those infrequent treats. Reference books were also shelved here since the one-room schoolhouse certainly did not have a separate library.

For this bookshelf, use ⅛-inch-thick wood, which is ¾ inch wide. Cut three pieces, each 2¾ inches long, for the shelves and two sides, each 2¼ inches long. Glue together as shown and stain and varnish when dry. For books, use different sized pieces of balsa wood, covering them with construction paper, leather, and even ribbon for a colorful effect. Glue onto the shelves and glue the shelf onto the wall.

Presidential Portraits

Every one-room schoolhouse had a picture of George Washington as the father of the country. Many also had a picture of Lincoln, and since Lincoln would have been President at this time, he is also pictured in this schoolhouse.

The portraits are from magazines and poster ads. These are 1½ inches wide by 2 inches high. The ones you use may be larger but not too much smaller for the proper effect. Glue the pictures to a piece of cardboard and let dry. For the frame, use ½-inch-wide balsa wood. The length of your pieces will depend on the size of your picture. For a perfect edge, overlap the corners of the balsa and cut through both pieces on the diagonal. Glue onto the picture with corners matching. Stain and varnish the frame and your portraits are ready to hang.

Presidential Portraits

Readers and Slates

The McGuffey reader, first published in 1836, was studied by generations of Americans who attended one-room schoolhouses. It taught reading through phonetics, and McGuffey's belief in self-reliance, honesty, kindness, and promptness was reflected in the reading material. Since paper was expensive, pupils often did their lessons on blackboard slates, although the older students were also taught penmanship on valued sheets of paper.

For the *McGuffey First Reader*, use 1/16 inch balsa wood and cut into pieces ⅝ inch wide by ¾ inch high. Cut pieces of brown construction paper 13/16 inch wide by 1½ inches long. Glue to the top of the balsa wood, leaving a small overlap on all sides. Using small squares of white paper, write *McGuffey First Reader* as small as possible and glue to the top. The *McGuffey Second Reader* is made the same way, except on a slightly larger scale. The balsa wood should be cut into pieces 1 inch high by ⅝ inch wide. Cover with green construction paper 1 1/16 inch wide by 1½ inch long. Glue title on as before.

For the slates, cut pieces of black matting board 1 inch long by ¾ inch wide. Round off the edges. Using ⅛-inch-wide balsa strips, cut two pieces each 1 inch long, and two pieces each ¾ inch long. Glue the 1-inch pieces to the two sides of the slate. Make a frame for the slate by laying the shorter pieces across the top and bottom, overlapping the edges. With an X-acto knife, cut through the two pieces of balsa wood on the diagonal, making an exact fit for the corners. Do all four corners this way and then glue the top and bottom pieces into place. With a piece of sandpaper, round off the edges to fit the matting

Readers and Slates

board underneath. Varnish the balsa wood. For writing on the slate, use white ink, and the tip of a round toothpick, painted white, is glued in place for the chalk.

Lunch Buckets and Baskets

One-room schoolhouses did not have our modern hot-lunch programs, and children brought their lunches from home in baskets or tin buckets. If the weather was nice, they could eat outside, but during the winter, they were forced to eat at their desks.

The girls often brought their lunches in small baskets similar to the one pictured. These are found in many toy and gift shops. Using material with a small print, fold the cloth in on itself to resemble lumpy contents and glue the ends into place.

For the lunch bucket, use a ½-inch dowel and cut to a length of ⅝ inches. With a small nail, make a small hole ⅛ inch from the top on opposite sides of the dowel. Paint the dowel silver. For the "lid," use black electrical tape and cut a circle to fit the top and a 1/16-inch strip for the side of the lid. For the handle, cut a piece of thin wire 1¼ inch long and bend into a semicircular shape. Bend the two ends toward one another and glue into the holes on the side of the dowel and you have your lunch bucket. The child's name may be painted on the side.

Lunch Buckets and Baskets

Hat and Coat Racks

Before one-room schoolhouses had a mud room, the coats, capes, and shawls were hung on simple racks in the schoolroom with a ledge provided for the hats and mittens.

Cut ¼-inch-wide balsa wood into three pieces, each 4 inches long. Next, cut a 4-inch length of ⅜-inch balsa wood. Glue the ⅜-inch-wide piece to the edge of one of the ¼-inch-wide strips for the hat rack. Stain and varnish all the pieces of wood. For the coat hangers, use tiny nails, seven in each row, spacing them so that the bottom row falls between the nails in the top row. Glue to the wall beside the stove. Small capes and scarves may be made to hang on the nails and tiny boots may be placed on the floor beneath them.

Hat and Coat Racks

Marbles, Slingshot, Pen, and Ruler

Even though the discipline was far more strict than it is today, children still found time to play during recess and after school and often brought equipment to school with them. A game of marbles was always a challenge although they were made of clay instead of glass. Proficiency with a slingshot was a sign of manliness, until you accidentally broke the schoolhouse window. Play equipment was often found on desks as were some other items needed for learning. There were inkwells with pens for the older students who could be trusted not to waste paper, and rulers were provided for making straight lines and certain math problems.

For the marbles, roll Repla-Cotta into tiny balls, bake, and paint white. The slingshot was made from a tiny fork in a branch. The greener the branch, the less likely that it will break. Use heavy weight thread for the "elastic" and tie to each branch, securing it with a drop of glue. A small piece of brown construction paper was glued into the middle of the thread for the stone to rest against. A small black bead was used for the inkwell. The pen is the pin you removed from the crystal pushpins that were used for glasses in the sweet shop. These inkwells may be glued into place, along with the marbles, since all have a tendency to move at the slightest jolt. The ruler is a ⅝-inch length of 1/16-inch-wide balsa wood. Make inch marks with a black felt-tipped pen.

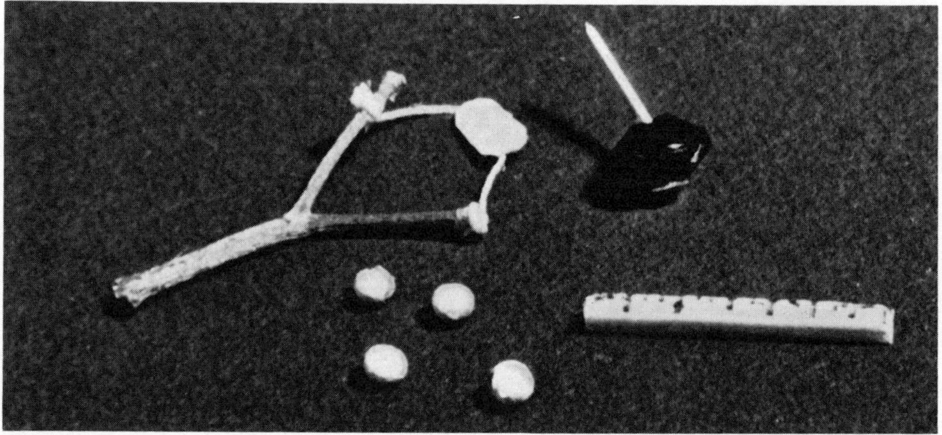

Marbles, Slingshot, Pen, and Ruler

Chart Holder

With little room in the schoolhouse, the teachers often had to improvise. They often built simple stands for helping them display the educational material. This stand might have been used for music sheets or world maps as well as pronunciation guides.

Use a dowel ⅛ inch in diameter. Cut a piece 3 inches long. For the base, use a power saw with a circle-making attachment if you have one (or else cut and sand into the shape of a circle) and make a base 1¼

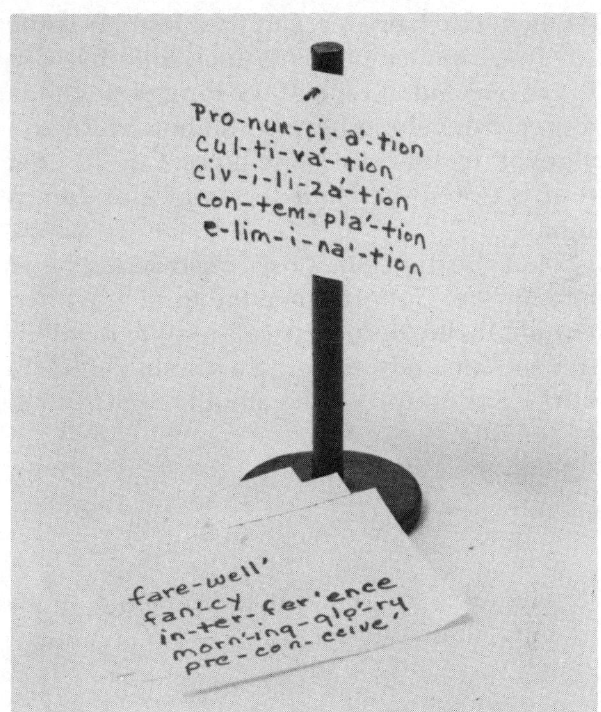

Chart Holder

inch in diameter. If you use the saw, you will have a hole in the middle of your circle. It will be slightly larger than your dowel. Use plastic Wood Dough to fill the hole around the dowel after you glue it into place. Hammer a small brad nail into the dowel ⅜ inch from the top. Paint the stand black. The charts should be 1¾ inches wide and 1¼ inches high. Make several. Make small holes in the middle of the charts and slip onto the nail. Place in front of the room and use your imagination to hear the children reciting by rote.

Dunce Stool and Hat

Education in the one-room schoolhouse was not kind to the child who did not learn easily. There was no special instruction for those with learning disabilities. Neither was there any mercy for those whose chores had prevented them from finishing their homework. The child was simply ordered to sit on the dunce stool and be an example to the whole class. The stools, often crude and handmade by the teacher, sat in front of the class as an eternal threat.

For this stool, use ⅛-inch-thick basswood. For the top, cut a circle

1¼ inches in diameter. Cut four legs 2⅛ inches long and ⅛ inch wide. Cut four smaller pieces ¾ inch long by ⅛ inch wide for the rungs. Taper one end of each of the long pieces. Make four small holes, each ⅝ inch from the other, in the bottom of the seat. Glue the tapered edges of the legs into these holes. Cut the edges of the rungs at a slant to fit between the chair legs and glue into place. Paint or stain the stool.

For the dunce hat, use construction paper. Make a semicircle 1¼ inches wide. Cut off one edge until you have 2 inches left across the bottom. Write *Dunce* vertically on the front of the paper and then fold over the two ends, forming a hat shape. Glue one on top of the other. Sit the hat on top of the stool to wait for the hapless student.

Dunce Stool and Hat

7

Shop Fronts

My father-in-law, John Duda, Jr., retired June 1, 1972, after spending a lifetime of work as a patternmaker. I am sure of the date because on his last day of work, he made a wooden planter and engraved the date on the bottom. That was to be his last piece of woodwork. It was at once a glad and sad occasion. I was glad to see that he would have more time to do the things he enjoyed but then again, I was sorry that we would see no more of his craftsmanship. I knew he was capable of fine work. I had seen the pembroke drop leaf end tables and the queen anne coffee table he had made my mother-in-law. Still, he insisted that he was going to relax after his retirement and for several years he kept his word. He traveled, watched the Watergate proceedings on television, and in general, seemed to enjoy relaxing—until 1974 when I wrote my first book on dollhouse accessories. He was intrigued, but it still seemed like child's play. Then I started this book in 1975 and he suddenly became interested in miniatures as an adult hobby.

"Do you need any help?" he finally asked. "I could make some of those things for you if it would help you."

That was the beginning. With little more than a carving knife (he had given all his tools to my husband years ago) and some basswood I had given him, he slowly started to make some of the things that were too hard for me. Little packages began to arrive and I found a butcher block for the general store or a piano for the confectionery. Every week seemed like Christmas and things were going fine, until my mother-in-law begged for more wood since he had cut the edge off her cutting board for one of the pieces!

More wood was ordered and hand tools were sent. My father-in-law was spending more and more time making things and my mother-in-law would keep us posted with notes such as: "Dad's taken over the kitchen table. The eating space keeps getting smaller and smaller."

Finally, we visited my father-in-law in late summer and I told him about some shop fronts I had seen at a miniature show.

"Give me some plans," he said, "and I'll make you some fronts."

That was all I needed. I started looking for pictures of fronts and redesigning ones I saw, or with my husband's help, creating our own fronts. My husband drew the blueprints and sent them to his father. These were very general, little more than basic measurements, and my father-in-law did the rest, improvising on the trims and doing all of the work by hand. My mother-in-law, an accomplished decorator, gave suggestions and assisted with items such as the draperies in the millinery.

General Store Front

Although each shop front is very individual, there are some basic similarities in the construction of each one. They were all made of ⅜-inch-thick plywood, for example, and ⅛-inch-thick basswood was used for the windows and doors. The doors do not open, but holes were cut for the windows and real glass was found more acceptable than plexiglass, which scratched easily.

The fronts were all assembled in a similar fashion. First, the plywood was cut for the front (approximately 25 inches wide and 11½ inches high, although this varied with the raised decorations or taller shingled roofs). Next, the holes were cut for the windows, including any windows above the doors. The doors and windows were then made. When the windows and doors were finished, a base piece was put on the bottom of the front. This piece was ½ inch thick and measured 4 inches deep and approximately 25 inches wide (this might vary if you are using shingles). Finally, the front was ready to be shingled (½-inch-wide strips of ⅛-inch-thick basswood) and decorated with moldings. Painting the shops brought out their real beauty. We tried to stay with colors of the period such as the Williamsburg blue on the millinery and the red on the toy shop. You may want to use a color to go with the color scheme of a certain room or you may want to stain the shops as we did the general store.

Looking more closely at the individual shops, you can see that tapered cedar shingles were used for the roof of the general store, which made it thirteen inches tall. We wanted an old, rough appearance to the store, so it was stained instead of painted. Looking at pictures of old general stores, we found that many had vertical siding, so random-width siding was individually glued onto the front of the store. This same pattern was used for the front porch. This shop front had the largest base, measuring 5½ inches deep and 26 inches wide. The porch was 4½ inches deep and the base extended ½ inch beyond the front and sides. The posts are ⅝ inch square. The double doors, including the frame and windows above, are 6 inches wide and 8 inches high. The windows are 5 inches wide and 5½ inches high. The window frames were painted white to set them off, and the sign was made with a woodburning tool. Benches and a knife sharpener adorn the porch, although many other things could go there and eventually will. There will be tools on the porch, and some late-arriving produce. Signs will be tacked on the doors and we might even have a couple of old codgers whittling on the benches. As I said in the first chapter, getting the basic store is only the beginning.

The toy shop has a recessed workshop area to break the line of the front. Like the others, the front was first made of ⅜-inch-thick plywood, but then the right side of the toy shop (16 inches) was added by gluing ⅝-inch-thick wood onto the ⅜-inch-thick piece. The bay window has five angles so that it looks curved although it is made with five vertical sheets of glass. The piece over the window was made from one solid piece of wood and carved with five angles to meet the window. The roof line has a greek key trim and there is siding on the whole front. There is quarter round around the base. One-half-inch

Toy Shop

dowels were used for the columns by the door and windows were cut above the door. With the columns, the door measures 4¾ inches wide and 9 inches high. The bay window is 7¼ inches wide with the trim and 8 inches high to the point. The small workshop window is 6 inches high and 4½ inches wide and there is an off-white shade in the window. The shop is painted red, the trim white, and the walk gray. This shop also has a sign, a drum made from ⅛-inch-thick basswood and hung with small chains from a dowel. A small dog waits outside for his young master, who must have ridden the tricycle.

The confectionery is the only front that did not have siding on it because it seemed to have so much decoration otherwise. The extended square display windows are 6 inches square. There are three rows of clear shelves for displaying the baked goods and sweets. Screen-door molding was used for the columns on the sides and on either side of the front door, which measures 6 inches wide, including the frame, and 9½ inches tall with the handcarved trim over the door. The brackets and trim were all handcarved and glued into place. There are windows in the doors and recessed trim on the bottom of the doors. There is a single step into the shop. The sidewalk was painted gray, the shop white, and the doors red (the same color that was used on the toy shop.) All of the doorknobs on the shops were purchased from dealers and painted gold.

In trying to make each shop different, we found this design for the millinery. In this case, the large display window is in the middle

Confectionery

with doors balancing it on either side. The window has seven panes of glass and the middle one is parallel to the front while the others are situated at an angle to it, giving the impression of being curved. The roof line also follows this pattern. The large window is 12 inches wide and 6 inches high. The doors are each 7½ inches high and 4½ inches wide. There are two steps leading to each one. The patterns on the door are handcarved, and ¾-inch dowels form the columns. The trim is different kinds of molding and there is a grill over the basement window. Williamsburg blue was used for this shop with white for the trim, frames, and steps. The walk was painted gray like the others. A small charm was used for decoration and the light blue curtains were hand-pleated.

With the schoolhouse, we found still another problem. Since the front of the box was really the side of the schoolhouse, we had to think of some way to break the flat, one-dimensional line of the side. We settled for a side door with a small porch and bell tower. To achieve this, we had to build up the roof line, and this front is 13½ inches high. The porch is 7 inches wide from the bottom step and 3½ inches deep. The two windows are 7 inches high (counting frames) and 4¼ inches wide, while the door is 7 inches high and 4 inches wide. The three roofs have cedar shingles and the sides have yellow clapboard siding, which extends beneath the porch as well. There is a small bell in the bell tower for calling the children. The handrail and balusters

Millinery

One-Room Schoolhouse

are all hand carved, and the handrail and door were stained for variety. Artificial grass was used on the base with an earth-colored path. The log pile was added to help balance the front. The season here is obviously spring, but if you have a winter scene in your windows as we did, you may remedy this with cotton spread thinly over the roof, porch, etc. Christmas trim snow sprays may also be used for a more permanent effect. We left it spring for this picture since the cotton hid the basic architecture.

I have tried to list the basic differences of each shop and school front. These could be changed many times to meet other needs. These examples are only a few of the many possibilities in this fascinating hobby. For us, the shops are keepsakes and will eventually be heirlooms.

In the meantime, my father-in-law and I continue to look and dream. Not long ago, we attended a regional miniature show. We were just amazed at the number of people from all walks of life who are enjoying this hobby.

"I wish I could have started years ago," my father-in-law said, and I silently agreed. Still, I felt lucky that he started when he did because he contributed so much to this book, which evolved far beyond the original outline.

In closing, I can only wish that the ideas we have presented here may bring you as much enjoyment as they have brought to us, and may they also bring many other artists out of retirement.

Bibliography

Aiken, Charlotte Rankin. *Department Store Merchandising Manuals—The Millinery Department.* New York: The Ronald Press Co., 1918.

Carney, Mabel. *Country Life and the Country School.* Chicago: Row, Peterson and Co., 1912.

Clark, Thomas D. *Pills, Petticoats, and Plows.* Norman, Oklahoma: Univ. of Oklahoma Press, 1974.

Daiken, Leslie H. *Children's Toys Throughout the Ages.* New York: Praeger, 1953.

Dickson, Paul. *The Great American Ice Cream Book.* New York: Atheneum, 1972.

Foley, Daniel J. *Toys Through the Ages.* Philadelphia: Chilton Books, 1962.

Frandsen, J. H., and Arbuckle, W. S. *Ice Cream and Related Products.* Westport, Connecticut: Avi Publishing Co. 1961.

Gott, Philip, and Van Houten, L. F. *All About Candy and Chocolate.* Chicago: National Confectioners' Association of the United States, 1958.

Jacobs, Flora Gill. *A History of Dolls' Houses.* New York: Charles Scribner's Sons, 1953.

McClintock, Inez and Marshall. *Toys in America.* Washington: Public Affairs Press, 1961.

Patty, Virginia C. *Hats and How to Make Them.* Chicago & New York: Rand McNally & Co. 1925.

Van Kleeck, Mary. *A Seasonal Industry.* New York: The Russell Sage Foundation, 1917.

White, Gwen. *Antique Toys and Their Background.* New York: Arco, 1971.

Index

Albrecht V of Bavaria, Duke, 81
American Flexible Flyer, 78
Animal pulltoys, 74
Anne of Brittany, 119
Aristotle, 61
Asian nomads, 86
Augusta Dorothea, Princess, 11
Axe, 56

Baby houses, 87
Backgammon, 70
Ball, 89
Banjo, 52
Baseball, 79
Basic construction layout, 18
Baskets, 156
Bat, 79
Bell, Alexander Graham, 27
Bell Telephone System, 27
Benson, A.C., 13
Berry baskets, 41
Bias tape, 48
Bible, 30, 31, 50, 61
Blackboard, 142
Blocks, 77
Bolts of cloth, 46
Bon bons, 113
Bonnets, 130
Book of the Queen's Dolls' House, The, 13
Books, 50, 76
Bookshelf, 152
Boston, 79
Boxes, 45
Box of candy, 114
Boy's Own Book, 72
Bread, 108
Bread pan, 54
Bronze Age, 86
Brooms, 57
Brownies, 113
Butcher block, 37

Cakes, 106
Candied apples, 114
Candles, 50
Cans of food, 45
Carpet beater, 52
Cash register, 25
Catherine de Medici, 119
Charles VIII, 119
Chart holder, 158
Checkerboard, 42
Checkers, 70
China, Chinese, 61, 75, 82
Christian, 61, 78, 79
Cilley General Store, 30
Civil War, 144
Coat rack, 157
Confectionery, 93
Confectionery front, 164
Cookie cutters, 54
Cookies, 108
Coolidge, Calvin, 30
Cooper Union Museum, 11
Cotton, John, 76
Countertop desk, 39
Countertop vegetable bin, 40
Craftsman Wood Service Co., 18
Crandall toy factory, 78
Crates, 44
Crawford, Nancy, 121
Crayons, 71

Danish rings, 110

Dart board, 70
Dauphin, 11
da Vinci, 72
Decorated shadow box, 19
Depression, 93
Divider, 95
Doll, 87
Dollhouse with front, 81
Door, 28
Doubleday, Abner, 79
Doughnuts, 110
Dresser set, 54
Dressing table, 121
Dressing table bench, 122
Drum, 84
Duda, Jr., John, 161
Dunce hat, 159
Dunce stool, 159

Eclairs, 108
Edward V, 89
Egg baskets, 41
Egypt, Egyptians, 71, 74, 88, 89, 119
Empress Eugenie, 119
England, English, 61, 62, 70, 71, 77, 85, 119

Fairings, 61
Fans, 135
Farmer's Almanac, 31, 50
Feathers, 136
Felt hat, 127
Flag, 144
Flexible Wood-Trim, 19
Flour sacks, 42
Flowers, 136
Flyswatter, 59
Football, 79
France, French, 62, 131
Front desk, 149
Fudge, 116

General store, 30
General store front, 163
Germany, Germans, 63, 80
Gingerbread, 112
Glasses, 59
Gloves, 135
Greece, Greeks, 61, 70, 74, 77, 88, 119, 128
Gulliver's Travels, 76
Gumball machine, 105

Hat boxes, 126
Hat forms, 122
Hat rack, 157
Henry VIII, 119
History of Europe, 1500–1848, 143
Hobbyhorse, 82
Homer, 61, 70, 89
Hoyle, Edmond, 70

Ice cream parlor chair, 98
Ice cream parlor table, 96
Industrial Revolution, 66, 88
Iron, 52
Irving, Washington, 62
Isn't It?, 121

Jack-in-the-boxes, 73
Jars of candy, 46
Jewelry, 132
Jump rope, 83

Kites, 75
Knickerbocker History, 62

Lace, 48
Ladder, 25
Lamps, kerosene, 50
Leroy lettering set, 142
Lincoln, Abraham, 154
Littlefield, Henry, 143
Lollipops, 114
Long counter, 21
Long, William, 85
Lunch buckets, 156

McGuffey readers, 50, 146, 154, 155, 156
Mailbox, 38
Marbles, 71, 157
Marie Antoinette, 119
Mary, Queen of Scots, 119
Mayflower, 70
Meadowcroft Village, 140
Mesopotamia, 86
Metcalf, Betty, 131
Michelangelo, 72
Michton, Morris, 89
Middle Ages, 61, 88
Millinery, 119
Millinery front, 165
Mirror, 122
Moore, Dr. Clement C., 62
Mother Goose, 76
Mr. Punch, 73
Museum of the City of New York, 11

Namur, 83
Napoleon, 119

Narrow-brimmed hat, 129
Necklace, 54
Noah's Ark, 80

Old Sturbridge Village, 140
Open dollhouse, 87
Ox yoke, 60

Paddleball, 84
Paint box, 76
Paper bags, 57
Paper cutter, 37
Parasol, 134
Parasol rack, 126
Parcheesi, 70
Pastries, 108
Pastry boxes, 117
Pen, 157
Pennsylvania Dutch, 80
Pennsylvania Packet, 85
Perfume bottles, 54
Persia, 61, 74
Pharaohs, 61, 70
Piano, 102
Piano bench, 105
Pies, 114
Pilgrims, 70
Pillsbury, 42
Platform, 94
Plato, 61, 70
Potato masher, 59
Pot-bellied stove, 32
Presidential portraits, 154
Prohibition, 93
Puritans, 61, 119
Purse, 138

Readers, 154
Rear bench, 152
Register counter, 64
Ribbon rack, 132
Roanoke Island, 61
Robinson Crusoe, 76
Rocking horse, 85
Rome, Romans, 71, 77, 88
Roosevelt, Teddy, 89
Rope, 56
Rousseau, 73
Ruler, 157

Sailboat, 80
St. Clement, 127
St. Nicholas, 62
Salem witch trials, 62
Scales, 34
School desks, 150
Schoolhouse, 140
Schoolhouse front, 165
Schwarz, 81
Shake, 116
Shakespeare, 79
Shawl, 138
Shawl rack, 124
Shelf unit, 20
Shelf with paint cans, 68
Shovel, 56
Showcase, 23
Slates, 154
Sled, 78
Slingshot, 157
Small counter, 22
Smithsonian, 12, 93, 94, 140, 146
Socrates, 61, 82
Soda fountain, 99
Spiritual Milk for Boston Babes, 76
Spool of thread, 46
Stilts, 83
Stockings, 138
Stockton and Darlington, 90
Stohlman's Confectionery, 93, 94
Straw hats, 131
String holder, 37
Sundae, 116
Sunday toy, 80

Teacher's chair, 146
Teacher's desk, 146
Teacher's desk accessories, 146
Teddy bear, 89
Tiffany lamps, 101
Top, 77
Toy shop, 61
Toy shop front, 163
Toy shop window, 67
Tumbling clown, 82

Ur, 70

Vegetable cutter, 54

Wagon, 86
Wall clock, 25
Wall map, 143
Wall mirror, 100
Wall telephone, 27
Warner's Almanac, 76
Washboard, 48
Wedding cake, 111
Wheelbarrow, 91
Wide-brimmed hats, 128
Windmill, 77
Woodbox, 34

Wooden barrel, 42
Wooden train, 90
Wooden washtub, 48
Wood supply box, 66
Workbench, 64
World's Fair, 93

X-acto knife, 18, 42, 50, 96, 112, 155

Yarn, 48